THE SUDAN

OLIVER ALBINO

The Sudan
A SOUTHERN VIEWPOINT

With a Foreword by
ARNOLD TOYNBEE

Published for the
Institute of Race Relations, London
OXFORD UNIVERSITY PRESS
LONDON
1970

Oxford University Press, Ely House, London W.1

GLASGOW NEW YORK TORONTO MELBOURNE WELLINGTON CAPE TOWN
SALISBURY IBADAN NAIROBI DAR ES SALAAM LUSAKA ADDIS ABABA
BOMBAY CALCUTTA MADRAS KARACHI LAHORE DACCA
KUALA LUMPUR SINGAPORE HONG KONG TOKYO

Printed in Great Britain by
Billing & Sons Limited, Guildford and London

Foreword by Dr. Arnold Toynbee

This book deserves to receive attention. It is based on personal experience; the statements made in it are supported by detailed factual information; and, above all, it is written in temperate language and is inspired, so it seems to me, by a sincere desire to find the way to a settlement, by agreement, between the peoples of the Southern and the Northern Sudan.

The history which the book records is tragic, and so is the present situation which it describes. The war (for it now is a war) between the Southern and the Northern Sudanese is like the wars in Vietnam, in the Middle East, and in West Africa between the Ibos and their former fellow Nigerians. In each of these wars, the belligerents are unequal in military strength, yet the militarily stronger party is proving unable to win its war by gaining a decisive military victory that would enable it simply to impose its will. In the Southern Sudan, as in the other present war-zones, the militarily stronger belligerent is being frustrated by a combination of two things that tell in the weaker party's favour. One of these things is the difficulty of the terrain for combatants who are not at home in it; the other is the spirit of the weaker party. The weaker belligerent is determined not to succumb, and it has learned how to turn to account the military advantage that the terrain offers to it.

A war that is being waged in these frustrating circumstances might be interminable if the belligerents were to continue to fail to find any basis for agreement. An agreed settlement cannot be reached without forbearance and wisdom on both sides. The stronger party would have to recognize two unpalatable facts: first, that it is not strong enough to win an outright military victory, and, second, that even if it could win this, it would not have the resources for holding down its defeated adversary permanently. The stronger party would be better off if it renounced the attempt to subjugate its weaker opponent. The weaker party, on its side, would have to go to the utmost possible lengths in order to save its opponent's face; for the stronger party would find it hard to reconcile itself to retreating if a golden bridge were not built for it. The weaker party's minimum need is to be effectively master in its own house. It needs to be secure, for the future, against being oppressed and exploited by its opponent. If it could persuade its opponent to agree to terms that were going to give the weaker party this security in practice, then it would be politic for the weaker party to be content with the substance of independence and to make concessions about the form. For instance, it would be wise for it to sacrifice sovereignty and to accept a federal constitution on terms that would prevent the other party from making federalism a cloak for domination.

As between the Southern and the Northern Sudan, is some such settlement going to be mutually acceptable within the foreseeable future? If not, it looks as if the present hostilities are likely to continue for an indefinite time to come. The Northern Army has already lost control of the greater part of the South. It now holds only the larger Southern towns and the principal lines of communication. On the other hand, the Southern guerrilla fighters, who have now succeeded in clearing the Northerners out of most of the countryside, do not have either the weapons or the training that would be required for dislodging relatively well-armed regular troops from the key positions that they still hold. How long is this stalemate likely to last, and in what way is it likely to be overcome—if it is overcome eventually? These are questions that the present book does not, and cannot, answer. But the facts presented in the book do not offer hope of a speedy or happy issue out of the present impasse.

Unfortunately the present tragic enmity between the Southern and the Northern Sudanese has a long tragic history behind it, and the cumulative evil effects of this history cannot be undone easily.

The two parts of the Sudan are each other's next-door neighbours. Both parts lie within the basin of the Nile and its tributaries. Yet the greater part of the South has been insulated from the North, till not more than a century and a quarter ago, by the papyrus swamps through which the waters of the Bahr-el-Jebel and the Bahr-el-Ghazal have to force their way; and even these main waterways are clogged by the *sudd*: a barrier formed by floating blocks of matted vegetation. I have had a glimpse of the swamp and the *sudd* in travelling from Juba to Malakal by steamer. The physical insulation has been so effective that there has been a time-interval of about thirty-four centuries between the dates at which the Northern Sudan and the Southern Sudan were opened up.

The Northern Sudan was opened up as long ago as the six-teenth century B.C., when at least the northernmost part of it was incorporated in Pharaonic Egypt. Since then, the Northern Sudan has passed through many vicissitudes. It has been a dependency of Pharaonic Egypt; it has been an independent kingdom; it has exchanged the Pharaonic Egyptian culture, first for Christianity, and then, since the fourteenth century of the Christian Era, for Islam; in 1820 it lost its independence again to Egypt; it then recovered it for eighteen years under the Mahdiya, and then it lost it once more to an Anglo-Egyptian condominium (a formula for what was in reality British rule). Finally, the Northern Sudan recovered its independence once again after the Second World War, when Egypt renounced the form, and Britain the substance, of sovereignty there.

These changes in the fortunes of the Northern Sudan have been kaleidoscopic, yet, all through, with the sole exception of the brief interlude of the Mahdiya, the Northern Sudan has been in constant communication with the great world. On the other hand, the Southern Sudan remained insulated from the rest of the world, including its immediate neighbour, the Northern Sudan, during by far the greater part of this long age. The Southern Sudan was not opened up till the second quarter of the nineteenth century, and then its first experience of contact with other peoples was most unhappy. First under the nineteenth-century Egyptian régime and then under the Mahdiya, the Southern Sudanese were plundered and oppressed, and their principal despoilers and oppressors were their nearest neighbours, the Northern Sudanese. These neighbours had now broken through the insulating physical barrier, and they raided the Southern Sudan to collect ivory and to capture slaves. This first meeting between the Southern Sudanese and the outer world has left bitter memories in Southern Sudanese minds.

For the Southern Sudanese, the British régime (1899–1956) was a relatively happy chapter of the recent period of their history during which they have been at last in contact with the rest of the world. Yet, considering the sequel, neither the Southern Sudanese nor the British can look back with satisfaction to the period of British rule. British intentions towards the Southern Sudanese were honest and humane, but British policy was not self-consistent and was not far-sighted.

When British rule, under the formula of an Anglo-Egyptian condominium, had replaced the Mahdiya in the Sudan, the British did shield the Southern Sudanese from the oppression and exploitation that they had suffered during the second half of the nineteenth century. For instance, the British suppressed the slave-trade; they also restricted, in general, the activities of Northern Sudanese traders in the South; and, as soon as they could, they built up an Equatorial Corps of troops recruited from Southerners only. There were no Northern Sudanese troops in the South from 1918 until after the mutiny of the Southern troops and the widespread insurrection of the Southern population in 1955. But, beyond raising the Equatorial Corps, which was never a match for the Northern part of the Sudanese Army, the British did little towards helping the Southern Sudanese to learn how to hold their own in the modern world.

Considering that the Southern Sudan had been exposed to the modern world since the 1840s and had suffered cruelly from its helplessness to defend itself against being oppressed and despoiled, it ought surely to have been evident, from the start, that the British had a choice between three alternative policies. Either they must go on shielding the Southern Sudanese by continuing to govern the Sudan without any time limit, or they must give the Southern Sudanese the opportunity to learn as quickly as possible how to fend for themselves, or, as a third alternative, they must eventually leave the Southern Sudanese at the Northerners' mercy again. In the light of the past it was manifest that this third alternative was the least desirable of the three; yet this was what the British did do after the Second World War.

The consequences might not have been so bad as they have been if the British had intended, all along, to do this, and if they had shaped their policy with that objective always in view. If the South was to be re-united with the North eventually, the reunion would have been least painful for the South if the North had been given a free hand to assimilate the South while the British were still in power in both parts of the country. If reunion was the objective, the British ought to have encouraged the spread, in the South, of Islam and of the Arabic language. However, reunion did not become the British régime's policy till the eleventh hour, and meanwhile the British had taken steps that were bound to alienate the South from the North and to make the North resentful.

The British fostered the Southern tribal manners and customs and the Southern languages; and the foreign religion to which they did give a free hand in the South was not Islam, it was Christianity. Thus, when the British abdicated—and they did this rather abruptly—they left a mainly Arabic-speaking and entirely Muslim North confronting a South that was still mainly pagan but that was now led by a small missionary-educated Christian intelligentsia. Certainly the British had not deliberately planned to set North and South by the ears, but this has been the effect of their policy—or rather of their lack of policy in failing to look ahead. The British differentiated the Northern and the Southern Sudanese from each other without separating them from each other politically. This made it virtually inevitable that, if and when the British abdicated, the Northerners, being by far the stronger of the two sections of the Sudanese people, should attempt, as they have done, to assimilate the Southerners by force. This, in turn, has made it inevitable that there should be a Southern resistance movement.

Unhappily there is no authority in the world today that has either the right or the power to intervene between local contending parties, to do justice between them in so far as this is humanly possible, and to compel them to make peace on the basis of as just a settlement as can be worked out. In the present-day world, sovereignty is distributed among 125 local states. Each of these still has the sovereign right to make war on any of the others, and each of them, within its own frontiers, is an arena in which contending parties and mutually hostile communities try to settle—but usually fail to settle—their disputes by resorting to force. This is anarchy; and, in the present state of the world, the local anarchy in the Sudan can be ended only by the Sudanese themselves. Can the Northern and the Southern Sudanese arrive at a settlement on terms acceptable to both parties? This would require a degree of goodwill and wisdom that is very rare today.

November 1969

Contents

Preface

I had long contemplated to write a highly opinionated book on the Southern Sudan. This gradually gave way to the present book in which I have merely aimed at outlining events leading to the present South-North conflict. In order to claim the reader's appreciation of the Southern view for an independent African state, I have tried to explain the various stages of the struggle in the South. The South started off as a reformist party, demanding rapid economic and educational progress before a decision could be taken on her future. When this demand was frustrated, she moved on to demand a federal status so as to avoid a political domination by the North. She was caught in the first race, by the transfer of legislative powers to the Sudan in 1948, and in the second, by independence in 1956. The North's lack of faith in the Southern Sudanese largely accounts for their refusal to pay heed to the cries for a federal system— thus bringing about the very domination which the South had abhorred.

Some Southerners believe that the problem would have been solved with a federation. They may be right for two reasons: (i) probably all the Southern leaders at the time were genuine believers in a federal status for the South; (ii) For those who are all out for an independent South, a federation would have created a balance of powers which would have facilitated the transformation of the South from a federal to an independent state without so much loss of lives on both sides (although Biafra's case proves the contrary). The second reason was probably in the back of the minds of Northern politicians when they persistently stood against federation. Under present circumstances, the only bait that may bring the South halfway to meet the North is independence, so that cooperation can be achieved between equals, as is the case between Britain and the

Commonwealth countries, or France and the French community.

I have deliberately refrained from devoting a chapter to the religious aspect of the problem. This may seem a self-contradiction to those whom I have told time and again that any exposition of the Southern problem that does not mention religious persecution is incomplete. But I hope my readers will agree with me that the essence of the problem is political, and, to avoid any bias, we have to accommodate our own Southern Muslim community. Northerners do not choose between Muslims and Christians before they kill. Nevertheless, I hope I have dealt with the religious problem adequately, though in a dispersed way.

Writing from exile, I hope my difficulties in acquiring up-to-date, detailed information on the Southern Sudan will be appreciated. In fact, this book would not have been possible without the Khartoum Round Table Conference on the South in March 1965. Nearly all the documents used as sources of information in this book were made available then, and as an exile who had lived for nearly two years in a literary vacuum, no words can sufficiently express my gratitude to the Conference Secretariat.

My thanks are also due to Mr. Elia Lupe Baraba, who read the manuscript and informed me on certain dates and Sudan Government salary scales. For the rapidity with which this work was done, I will not forget Mr. Joseph L. Loro who typed the first manuscript, and Mrs. Toshi Taylor, who retyped the revised script as it appears in this book.

Above all, this book has become a reality due to my friends Ken McVicar and his wife, Jan McVicar. On reading my letter to His Excellency, Mzee Jomo Kenyatta, they felt that I should write 'something simple and understandable by the ordinary man'. When I was ultimately persuaded to do so, I proceeded to use the same letter as the basis of my research. They also read the manuscript, and offered a number of very encouraging suggestions.

Any part of this book which may still appear impassionate is due to my stubbornness to sustain certain convictions, and for this, I hope my friends who had suggested other forms of presentation will not take offence.

OLIVER ALBINO

The Sudan and Neighbouring Countries

1 | The South and its People

The Sudan is a country of almost one million square miles whose three southern provinces, Bahr el Ghazal, Upper Nile, and Equatoria, constitute what is known as the South. The geographical, climatic, and ethnic differences between the South and the rest of the country are considerable, and have given rise to political opposition between the two parts which it will be the main task of this book to describe. This first chapter starts with a brief summary of physical and cultural features of the South.

The key to the difference between South and North is rainfall. This varies enormously within the Sudan. At the extreme north, on the boundary with Egypt, there is practically no rainfall. Six or seven inches fall at Khartoum, twelve at El Obeid in the west, thirty-five at Malakal and Juba, forty-four at Wau, and fifty on the south-west border. Correspondingly, vegetation in the North is either non-existent or of the arid type, except where irrigation is possible along the banks of the Nile and in the area between the Blue and White Niles known as the Gezira. Vegetation in the South, on the other hand, ranges from vast grassy plains to lush tropical forests on the Nile-Congo watershed. The agricultural possibilities of the North are limited by the scope of irrigation, while those of the vast, well-watered South have barely been surveyed.

The geography of the South has been compared to an enormous shallow saucer, tilted towards the North. Along the southern half of its rim the land rises to the borders of the Central African Republic, the Congo (Kinshasa), Uganda, Kenya, and Ethiopia, with a gap through which flow the incoming waters of the White Nile (Bahr el Jebel). The land to the west of the Bahr el Jebel is drained by the Bahr el Ghazal, that to the east by the Sobat, and all these rivers flow into a huge, flat, clay plain at the base of the saucer. There the water either floods over the impermeable clay during the rainy season, leaving the inhabitants perched on marshy islands of high ground, or collects in enormous papyrus swamps, where the rivers are frequently blocked by masses of floating vegetation known as *sudd*. The outlet of this basin is to the north, where that water which has not been lost through evaporation flows in a leisurely fashion down the Nile to Khartoum.

Generally speaking, the people of the Northern Sudan may be described as Arab and Islamic; those of the South as negroid and pagan, with a certain proportion of Christians. (There are exceptions to this rule in the North, the most notable being the Nuba and the Fur, who are of predominantly negroid origin with little Arab blood.) The peoples of the South fall into three main groups: Nilotic, Nilo-Hamitic, and Western Sudanic.

The Nilotes comprise the Dinka, Nuer, and Luo people. The Dinka are divided into a number of distinct sub-tribes (for example, the Cic, Bor, Aliab, Agar, Atot) who in the past frequently feuded among themselves, only uniting against a common enemy on rare occasions. They occupy the largest territory of any tribe in the South, avoid tilling the land, and attach themselves to their cattle with a single-minded devotion which leads every young Dinka boy to effect what amounts to a complete psychological identification with a particular ox or bull.[1] The Nuer are also devoted cattle-raisers. The country they inhabit lies deeper into the swamps than that of the Dinka, and their isolation from outside influences has contributed to their characteristic pride and independence. The distribution of the Luo people is more complex. They appear to have divided long ago

---

[1] C. G. and B. Z. Seligman, *Pagan Tribes of the Nilotic Sudan* (London, 1932), contains a wealth of anthropological information on the Southern Sudan, as do E. E. Evans-Pritchard's *Witchcraft, Oracles and Magic Among the Azande* (London, Oxford University Press, 1937), and *The Nuer* (London, Oxford University Press, 1956).

into two branches, one of which moved north and gave rise to the Shilluk and Anuak people, while the other turned south and became the ancestors of the Acholi and other tribes in northern Uganda. The Shilluk have a higher degree of social organization than any other tribe in the Sudan, with the possible exception of the Azande, their king or *reth* being a head of state whose authority is both temporal and spiritual. The *reth* is in fact regarded as divine, a tradition which may derive from ancient Egypt, and his office is heavy with ritual meaning.

The Nilo-Hamites, as their name suggests, are supposed to contain more Hamitic blood than their neighbours, although this view is disputed by those who prefer to speak of them as 'Eastern Nilotes'. They include the Bari, Lotuko, Lokoya, and Dongotono on the east bank of the Nile, and the Mundari, Kuku, Kakwa, Pöjulu, and Nyangwara on the west. Among these Bari-speaking peoples there is not the degree of social organization seen among the Shilluk; tribal affairs are run by councils of elders, although special significance is attached to the hereditary rain-making chiefs. They both cultivate the land and keep cattle.

Finally, the extreme south-western part of the country is inhabited by people speaking Sudanic languages, who entered from the Congo river basin in successive waves. Early invasions resulted in the establishment of the Kreish, Bongo, Moru, and Madi tribes, while later ones produced the powerful Azande group. These people, ruled over by their class of chiefs known as the *Avungara*, were notable, especially in the nineteenth century, for the degree of social cohesion which the power of these chiefs produced. The Zande live in tsetse fly country, which prohibits the keeping of cattle, and are hence exclusively cultivators.

RACIAL DIFFERENCES

Racial differences constitute the root of the problems which beset the Sudan. According to the 1956 Census, the population of the Sudan was 10,231,507, distributed as follows:

Arabs	39%
Southerners (Africans)	30%
Western Sudanese (Africans)	13%
Nuba (Africans)	6%
Beja (African origin)	6%
Nubians (Hamitic type)	3%
Others	3%

Nevertheless, it would be ridiculous to suppose that multiracialism, from a purely ethnic point of view, could have caused such a state of mutual intolerance. As Robert E. Park rightly points out, a racial problem cannot exist unless there is 'a consciousness of individuals to differences between their racial groups',[2] and this consciousness is almost invariably provoked by the ruling race which has the monopoly of power. The subject race, as Edgar T. Thompson puts it, is simply 'one whose members are treated as such, believe themselves to be such, and behave as such. The *race* and the *relation* seem to be born together.'[3] It is only in this perspective that we can appreciate the problem between the Africans of the Southern Sudan and the Arabs of the Northern Sudan. It is a problem of unhealthy if not hostile *relations* which has influenced all contact between the two races.

But the existing conflicts cannot be explained solely in terms of race relations. These relations existed before independence, and yet there were no clashes between the Africans and the Arabs, simply because they were kept at arm's length from each other by those who wielded political power. Since the Sudan became independent, the Arabs took power from the British, and, because of bitter memories of the past on both sides, sought to behave in a manner which they believed would frighten Southerners into submission. They have a complete monopoly over economic, social, educational, administrative, and military affairs. In short, the Arabs run the whole machinery of government. The South, on the other hand, is a colony. To understand the facts subsequently outlined, one must first separate the

[2] In E. Thompson (ed.), *Race Relations and the Race Problem: A Definition and an Analysis* (Durham, North Carolina), Duke University Press, 1939).
[3] Ibid.

South and the North, not only as distinct geographical entities, as they actually are, but also as sharply defined human societies—the governed and the governors, or the slaves and the masters.

Paradoxically, the Arab administrator feels and behaves more like a foreigner in the South than did the British. He goes about his job as if he were there partly to tame the people, and show them that the very meaning of authority lies in the Arab race, and partly to make the greatest personal profit out of his office. As a result, he appears to the African in the South to lack self-confidence, and only behaves cruelly in self-assertion. References such as 'our government has done more for you than the former British Government' leave little doubt in the minds of the Africans that they are only a subject race. There is no doubt that this type of relationship breeds more mutual hatred, and the Arab determination to cling to power cannot be regarded as having any ethical motivation. In the words of Edmund Burke: 'Those who have been once intoxicated with power, even though but for one year, can never willingly abandon it.' This goes a long way to explain why, even with the very best intentions, no Arab Government will consciously devote its time to a development programme in the South that may result in a seizure of power by the Africans. The latter are already definitely committed to the slogan of the right to self-determination.

The cry by Southerners for political freedom brings us to the other side of the problem. The Africans of the Southern Sudan have not only realized the need to retain their identity and dignity, but see a clear-cut difference between their aspirations and those of the Arabs. The Arabs aspire to Arab nationalism and the universal brotherhood of Islam, while the Africans of the South feel they must have the chance to make their humble contribution to the growth of African nationalism and Pan-Africanism. Whatever idea may be held about the Northern Sudanese, the fact remains that they call themselves Arabs—maybe from a purely political point of view—and are very proud to do so. They feel hurt when they are denied this name which has become highly emotive throughout the Middle East. In the words of Mr. Ali Abdel Rahman, then Minister of Interior in a People's Democratic Party (P.D.P.)–Umma coalition: 'The Sudan is an integral part of the Arab world, and as such, must accept the leadership of the two Islamic leaders of the Sudan [Sayed Ali El Mirghani and Sayed Abdel Rahman El Mahdi—now Sayed Sadiq El Mahdi]. Anybody dissenting from this view must quit the country.'[4]

Politically then, the Northern Sudanese look towards the Arab Middle East as the home of their Pan-Islamic culture and political aspirations. Southerners, on the other hand, look towards the rest of Africa as their kith and kin, with many similarities in their social and cultural outlook. The conflict that has arisen is due to the fact that the Arab policy of political assimilation is clearly not aimed at a union between equals, but is calculated to nip African aspirations in the bud in order to upgrade Arab nationalism. Political conditions in Zanzibar prior to the revolution clearly indicate how difficult it is for an Arab to live side by side as an equal with an African, especially when he has tasted power.

Dr. Nkrumah once warned that Africa must be aware of expansionist designs emanating from within. The time has gone when we all feared European or white imperialism. We must not be misunderstood by Africans simply because of the Organisation of African Unity. As long as we remain in political bondage, it will be impossible to appreciate our desire to contribute towards African unity. One thing is however clear: to sacrifice four million black Africans to the Arabs on the altar of African unity may defeat the purpose of unity itself. Ours is not just a case of territorial integrity or an internal affair. When the whites designed federation in 1953 for the Rhodesias and Nyasaland, the main reason, I believe, was that they wanted an outward flow of the philosophy of white supremacy from Southern Rhodesia

[4] *Parliamentary Proceedings: second sitting of the first session of parliament*, 1958, p. 3. Sayed Ali El Mirghani is the leader of the Khatmia religious order and patron of the P.D.P. Sayed Sadiq El Mahdi is the head of the Ansar sect and hereditary president of the Umma Party.

instead of an inward flow of the comparatively liberal policy towards blacks that existed in Northern Rhodesia (now Zambia) and Nyasaland (Malawi). The African leaders realized this, and fought hard against federation until it was finally broken in 1963. With so much resentment from the Organization of African Unity for Mr. Ian Smith's unilateral declaration of independence, one would ask: What would have been the cry if it were Sir Roy Welensky who had decided to seize power as the federal Prime Minister of the Central African Federation? To understand the situation in the Southern Sudan, imagine a situation where the Central African Federation existed as an independent state, with all the evils of apartheid emanating from the capital of Salisbury to tighten the grip of the whites upon Zambia and Malawi. Would the Africans still describe this as an internal affair, and pledge to respect the territorial integrity of the Federation? The Republic of South Africa, which is not a hypothetical case, faces a great deal of criticism from the world as well as from the Organization of African Unity. This reveals a resentment of discrimination against man by man. If the O.A.U. seeks to promote the unity as well as the welfare of the Africans, then the case of the Southern Sudanese deserves attention.

To accept our situation would be to spread the problem along the Nile Valley, and eventually into all Black Africa. We cannot resign ourselves to such a fate. Nationalisms can co-exist. But to try to suppress one in favour of another is, I think, to venture upon an impossible task. Yet many, including the Arabs, would not only like to suppress African nationalism, but are quite consoled with the assumption that it is non-existent, and anyone trying to assert it must therefore be equated with a trouble-maker. What in fact is happening today is that Arabs are actively engaged in paying lip-service to the cause of African unity only in order to dilute any effort by the Black African states from within, so that they cannot become a strong power bloc. Having lived with the Arabs in the Sudan, and listened to their views, I am left in no doubt that real Arab allegiance is paid to the Arab League and not to the O.A.U. I appreciate the O.A.U. as it stands. But what I feel is that Black African states should have an organization of their own, like the Arab League—call it the African League—to promote understanding between them, and, above all, to give back to Pan-Africanism the impetus with which it started. The O.A.U., as it is today, could then be a superstructure through which the views of the Africans as well as those of the Arabs could be reconciled.

I know how daring these suggestions are because, on attaining independence, African politicians tend to abandon their individual spectacles to look at the world through a universal windscreen. All I need say is that we need a husband and a wife to start a family, and that we need a number of families to form a tribe or a nation. It is only when society is built on these humble foundations that claims can be made for the good of the whole.

We may all condemn Dr. Vorster's régime in South Africa, Mr. Smith's unilateral declaration of independence, or the Salazar policies in Angola and Mozambique. But we need to be made aware of still another type of oppression which is equally retarding to African progress. If we look at the situation that prevailed in Zanzibar, many would be inclined to dwell on the argument that it was the creation of imperialists. In the Southern Sudan today, too much time is wasted on blaming the problem on the 'British imperialists' instead of making an effort to solve it. As to the question, 'Who caused the problem?', the answer is not as simple as 'the British', or 'imperialists'. All the succeeding pages seek to pin-point the cause.

II | The History of the Sudan

IVORY AND SLAVES

Just as the modern history of Egypt begins with its conquest by Napoleon in 1798, so the modern history of the Sudan begins with its conquest by Egypt in 1820–1. Muhammad Ali, having subdued the Nubian riverain tribes and the once-powerful Funj Kingdom of Sennar, founded Khartoum in 1824. In due course he turned his attention to the South, and in 1839 dispatched Salim, a Turkish naval captain, to sail up the White Nile from Khartoum. By early 1841 Salim had reached Gondokoro, near the present Juba, and for the first time a route from the north into the heart of Central Africa was opened.

Salim's journey of over 1,000 miles is worth recounting. It took him first into Shilluk country, and later between Shilluk on the west bank and Dinka on the east. South from Kaka, an unbroken line of villages stretched along the grassy west bank, and friendly contact was made with the people, though the *reth* (king) would not be interviewed. Farther south, the travellers saw the last tongues of firm ground fall behind them as they entered the vast papyrus swamp beyond the junction of the Sobat. Turning west and then south, they encountered only isolated fishing villages of Nuer and Cic Dinka until, 300 miles later, the banks became solid again and they were able to collect firewood in the Bor Dinka country. Having returned to Khartoum for supplies, they proceeded southwards the following year and entered Bari country. Sailing upstream through fine parkland, and accompanied by crowds of welcomers dancing on the banks, the party reached Gondokoro, beyond which the

river became too swift for navigation. Having ascertained
that the area was rich in ivory, and that the Bari were well
disposed to bartering it for beads, the expedition returned
in triumph to Khartoum.

The European traders in that town were not slow to
realize the potentialities of Salim's discovery. Soon they
began to embark on trading expeditions to the south.
Between 1851 and 1856 the quantity of ivory collected rose
from 400 quintals (20 tons) to 1,400 quintals, annually, this
being obtained for beads worth less than a hundredth of
its value.

All did not go smoothly, however, with the process of
bartering. At first the ivory was obtained near the river.
But as these sources became exhausted, more strenuous
methods of collection were needed. Expeditions were sent
many days' march inland from the river, and hundreds of
tribesmen were conscripted to act as porters. Each trader
maintained a number of armed Arab servants, and the
behaviour of the latter to the Southerners laid the foundations
of all future mistrust and hatred between South and North.

'It is indisputable that the prevalent attitude of scorn
towards the savage, naked "abids" [slaves], which then
existed in the northern Sudan, has been one of the most
important and disastrous influences governing the contact
of the southern Sudan with the outside world.'[1]

On even the earliest expeditions it had been the practice
for the Arab soldiers to buy or seize one or two slaves each,
to be sold later in Khartoum. But with the advent of large-
scale sorties into the interior, the importance of slavery grew,
so that eventually it overshadowed the ivory trade.

The first of the European traders systematically to exploit
the interior was a Frenchman, de Malzac, who by 1856
owned a trading station eight days' march westward from
the Bahr el Jebel (White Nile) at Rumbek and needed 500
tribesmen to carry his ivory to the river. He devised the
method of obtaining ivory by *razzias* or cattle raids on the

[1] R. Gray, *A History of the Southern Sudan, 1839–1889* (London, Oxford
University Press, 1961), p. 36. Most of the information in this and the next
section comes from this source.

local tribes, some of the cattle being used for food and the rest exchanged for ivory. Women and children taken in these *razzias* were sold to de Malzac's soldiers. De Bono, a Maltese, combined the ivory trade with open slave-dealing, playing off one tribe against another to obtain captives; and in 1860 it was reported that one of his boats set off for Khartoum with no fewer than 550 slaves, most of whom, however, died in transit. In the Bahr el Ghazal, which had been opened up to navigation in 1856 by the British Consul Petherick's discovery of a route west through the papyrus to Meshra er Rek, the situation was much the same. The country was divided up among the Sudanese, Syrian, and Egyptian traders, who established themselves in forts or *zeribas*, and pillaged small tribes such as the Kreish, Bongo, and Jur who lived between the more intractable Dinka and Azande. By 1870, the slave trade was estimated to be 12,000 to 15,000 slaves per annum, most of whom were exported northwards, overland to Kordofan or Darfur.

ISMAIL'S ERA

The outside world was not, however, content to let this slave trade flourish unchecked. Ismail, who became Khedive of Egypt in 1863, was a 'westernized' ruler willing, partly under pressure from anti-slave sentiment in England and elsewhere, to take steps to abolish it. Reports on slavery were received from the European consuls at Khartoum and from Roman Catholic missionaries who had established a station at Gondokoro as early as 1853, but had later been forced to withdraw, partly because of difficulties witht he Bari and partly because of the climate. More important, however, was the account given to Ismail by the explorers Speke and Grant, who in 1863 returned from Lake Victoria via the Nile. Their report conjured up visions of the river serving as a highway for trade with the prosperous kingdoms of Bunyoro and Buganda in the interior, and Ismail's ambitions were aroused. Deciding to extend Egyptian authority in the area, he began by trebling the tax on White Nile commerce. This, however, merely resulted in the withdrawal of all European traders and their replacement by others, such as the Egyptian Muhammad al 'Aqqād, who were if anything more ruthless. But Ismail persevered and in 1869 persuaded Sir Samuel Baker, who five years earlier had discovered Lake Albert, to lead a major expedition up the Nile.

The objects of Baker's expedition were modest: to crush the slave trade, to encourage agriculture among the native peoples, to open the equatorial lakes to steam navigation, and to bring the whole Nile basin under Egyptian sovereignty. None of these aims was accomplished. Baker was delayed for a year by the *sudd*, and when he reached Gondokoro he found the Bari, after thirty years' contact with the outside world, not only unwilling to improve themselves by agriculture but reluctant even to sell their cattle for meat. Baker was forced to adopt the methods of the hated ivory traders and resort to a *razzia*. Then, owing to the hostility of the people, he was unable to transport his three dismantled steamers to above the cataracts at Bedden. When he eventually continued southwards on foot he encountered the opposition of Abū Su'ūd, 'Aqqād's representative, who was informed by Baker that with the arrival of the Egyptian flag his master's monopoly on slaves and ivory had ended, and that his elaborate chain of forts at Faloro, Patiko, Foweira, and so on was now Government property. Having fought with practically everyone, including Kabarega, King of Bunyoro, Baker returned home, informing the world that he had stamped out slavery on the Nile, but in fact leaving the situation in the Southern Sudan much as he had found it.

Meanwhile, in the Bahr el Ghazal another expedition of Ismail's, sent in 1869 to bring the area under Egyptian control, fared even less well. The largest slaver in the district was a Ja'li Sudanese Arab, al-Zubair, who by dint of marrying the daughter of an Azande chief had built up an empire which extended well over the Nile-Congo watershed. By 1866 he was judged to be exporting about 1,800 slaves annually, which at the rate of £E8 each at Khartoum were worth £E14,400 compared with only £E2,300 worth of ivory. Zubair defeated Ismail's expedition, whereupon Ismail shrewdly countered by appointing him to his admini-

stration as Governor of Bahr el Ghazal. Zubair eventually
fell out with Ismail, however, and was put under house-
arrest in Cairo, but his son Sulaiman continued to be a
thorn in the flesh of Ismail's next representative, C. G.
Gordon.

Like Lawrence of Arabia, Gordon was a combination of
soldier and mystic. During his term as Governor of Equatoria
Province, from 1873 to 1876, his habit of introspective
thought enabled him to assess the influence of 'civilization'
on the Southern Sudan more accurately than any of his
predecessors. At that time the largest number of outsiders
in the country were Danaqla (Dongolese). These people had
no official status, but lived off the land, had become thoroughly
acclimatized to the South, and traded and behaved as they
pleased. Gordon was often forced to accept the Danaqla as
allies in his dealings with the hostile and embittered tribesmen, but he wrote:

If *we* conquered the country we would at least in some measure
benefit the conquered; but here I cannot say I see the least chance
of the country being improved or the people benefited; the
civilizers are so backward themselves that they cannot be expected
to civilize others. [2]

In an even more characteristic mood, however, Gordon saw
the futility of attempts to 'improve' people in the absence
of any understanding of their life and social customs.
Western civilization was not the answer, either for the
tribes, or for the half-caste retinue, speaking pidgin Arabic,
who surrounded the camps of the soldiers and traders.
'I feel it would be better for [Arabs and Southerners] to
work out the problem of how to live together by themselves.'[3]
It is in musings such as this, rather than in his building of a
chain of posts linking Khartoum with Foweira, his surveying
of the Nile as far as Lake Kyoga, or his launching of two
steel boats on Lake Albert, that Gordon's particular genius
is to be sought.

Persuaded by Ismail, Gordon returned as Governor of

---

[2] Quoted in B. M. Allen, *Gordon and the Sudan* (London, 1931), p. 61.
[3] Quoted in Gray, op. cit., p. 112.

the Sudan from 1877 to 1880, but he left the actual administration of the South to a German and an Italian, Eduard Schnitzer (Emin Pasha) in Equatoria, and Romolo Gessi in the Bahr el Ghazal. Following the signing of the Anglo-Egyptian Slave Trade Convention in 1877, the stamping out of slavery had become Gordon's principal aim. Gessi was dispatched to deal with Zubair's son Sulaiman, under whom the slave route from the Bahr el Ghazal northwards through Darfur had come to completely overshadow that up the Nile. In 1879 Gessi defeated and killed Sulaiman, and there followed a period of calm, during which Gessi introduced some remarkable innovations. Amongst the Kreish, Bongo, and Jur Luo, Gessi found many who were delighted to escape from the fear of slave raids and adopt a life of collecting rubber and cultivating cotton. Eight looms, worked by young Southern Sudanese, produced cotton cloth. Honey, rubber, and tamarinds were exported to Khartoum. A primary school was established at Dem Zubair, Zubair's former headquarters. By this success, Gessi demonstrated that the problems imposed by the slave traders could be solved by the development of agriculture and local industries, and his lead was followed in the east by Emin. The latter was a doctor and naturalist, a convert to Islam, who made Equatoria his home. He introduced the cultivation of coffee, rice, tobacco, nutmeg, and indigo, tried to breed cattle which were immune to tsetse fly, and laid out neatly planned towns, each with a public garden. He built a Koranic school and a hospital in his capital, Lado. His soldiers were mostly Makaraka tribesmen, as were some of his officers. There is little doubt that, given time, Gessi and Emin could have broken for ever the deadly sway of ivory and slaves over the Southern Sudan. But their efforts were all undone by the Mahdi.

THE MAHDIYA

It was the belief of the Sanūsi Community (a muslim religious order founded about 1830) that a 'Mahdi' or Messiah would appear at the beginning of the thirteenth Islamic century (in 1301, i.e. 1883). In actual fact it was in

1881 that Muhammad Ahmad, the son of a Dungula boat-builder, declared himself the Mahdi. In the course of four stunning victories over the forces of the Egyptian administration the Mahdi's followers (the Ansar) grew rapidly in number, support being found especially among the merchants and slave traders whose business had suffered through taxes and Government intervention. Lupton, Gessi's successor in the Bahr el Ghazal, was engaged in a full-scale war against the Dinka and eventually, despite help from the Zande Chief Zamoi, was forced to surrender in 1884 by the Mahdists under Karam Allah. But the overthrow of the Egyptian régime did not give the tribes of the region the freedom they desired, for the coming of the Ansar was the signal for the slave traders to resume operations. However, in 1885 Karam Allah's army left the Bahr el Ghazal, and traditional life was able to re-establish itself in that area until the Anglo-Egyptian régime in the twentieth century.

The fall of Khartoum and the death of Gordon[4] came in 1885, leaving only Equatoria untouched by the Mahdi's armies. But Equatoria never fell. Karam Allah was able to take Amadi on the Yei river only with considerable trouble, and upon the death of the Mahdi late in 1885 withdrew. Under the Khalifa, the successor to the Mahdi, another expedition nearly succeeded in conquering Equatoria, the leadership of the province having been seriously weakened by Emin Pasha's indecision as to whether to abandon the area and accompany Stanley's 'Emin Pasha Relief Expedition' to Zanzibar. Emin did eventually leave in 1889, but one of his officers, Fadl al-Mula, stayed on and contained the Mahdists' thrust to Lake Albert. To their disappointment, the latter made no religious impact upon the pagan people of the South, who remained either indifferent or actually hostile to Mahdism, and the Khalifa's troops had to raid the countryside continually for supplies. This fact, and their general inability to establish any permanent co-existence or *modus vivendi* with the tribes, accounts for the extremely

---

[4] After leaving the post of Governor, Gordon was appointed in 1884, at the height of the Mahdist revolution, to try to effect the withdrawal of Egyptian troops and citizens from the Sudan.

disruptive influence of the Mahdist State on the peoples of the South.[5]

The stage leading to final defeat of the Ansar in Equatoria began in 1893, when Congolese soldiers belonging to King Leopold of Belgium appeared in the Southern Sudan. Leopold was anxious to annex the territory to the west of the Nile, and his troops allying themselves both with Fadl al-Mula and with Zamoi, were eventually successful, defeating the Khalifa's General 'Arabi at the battle of Rejaf in 1897. Subsequently, Leopold was allowed to administer as part of the Congo a section of the Southern Sudan known as the 'Lado enclave', banded by the Nile, 5°30' north and 30° east. Following Leopold's death in 1909, the Lado enclave reverted to the Sudan.

Meanwhile, in the North the British, spurred on by reports that the French were attempting to gain a foothold on the Upper Nile, were marching on Khartoum under General Kitchener. In the battle of Omdurman on 2 September 1898, the Khalifa's forces were decisively defeated, and a fresh chapter in the history of the Sudan opened with the declaration of a new government—the Anglo-Egyptian Condominium.

THE EARLY YEARS OF CONDOMINIUM RULE IN THE SOUTH

By an agreement signed on 19 January 1899, Great Britain and Egypt became the co-rulers of the Sudan.[6] In practice, however, it was the British alone who ruled in the South; all ranks down to and including Assistant District Commissioner being Britons. The first task facing the administration in the South was to re-establish communications, which in the later years of the Mahdiya had been almost totally obstructed by the *sudd*. This was accomplished by 1903. The next task was the imposition of the Pax Britannica upon a land that had not known peace since the coming of the ivory traders, and this occupied the Government for the

[5] See R. O. Collins, *The Southern Sudan 1883–1889* (New Haven, Yale University Press, 1962), pp. 72 f.

[6] For the text of the agreement, see Beshir M. Said, *The Sudan* (London, Bodley Head, 1956), pp. 156 f.

best part of twenty or thirty years. Many of the tribes regarded every man's hand raised against them, and simply ran away when outsiders came in sight. Others were ruled by chiefs who vowed to resist to the death any incursions by foreigners. All wanted to be left alone.

Faced with this problem the natural administrative policy was simply for Government officers to be *seen*, i.e. to travel quietly through the countryside without raiding, accompanied either by troops or by a policeman and an interpreter only. At times, force had to be used, as for example against the Zande chief, Yambio, an Avungara chief whose ancestors, conquering the Zande, had since ruled despotically over them. He held life and death powers over his people and refused to submit to the Government. So in 1904 a military patrol was sent against him, and he was killed. Another case in which force was used was that of Gwek Wondeng, the Nuer prophet. Gwek was an epileptic whose fits inspired him to prophecy and to defiance of the administration. He was finally killed in 1927 by the army in the shadow of the mysterious pyramid of Dengkur, led on to battle together with 300 warriors by Bimerol, his sacred bull.[7]

During the first years in the South the soldiers used were Northern Sudanese. But in 1911 the training began of a local Equatorial Corps which by 1918 had entirely replaced the Northern army in the South. These Southern troops were regarded by the British as a valuable counterweight to Arab (and Egyptian) influences in the Sudan, and they continued to be the sole military force in the South until replaced by Northern units following the 1955 mutiny and subsequent uprising.

The early years of Condominium rule were also marked by the return of missionaries to the South—Roman Catholics to the Shilluk in 1901, American Presbyterians to the Sobat river in 1902, and the Church Missionary Society (C.M.S.) to Malek in 1905. To control the missions' activities and rivalries, the Government assigned each of these religious denominations a 'sphere of influence', with all the sad

[7] H. C. Jackson, *Sudan Days and Ways* (London. 1954), p. 170.

c

consequences that such a division implied.[8] But if it were not for the churches, there would have been no education in the South. By 1926, there were twenty-two boys' elementary schools, nine girls' elementary, two boys' intermediate, and one boys' trade school, in addition to numerous village vernacular schools. English was the medium of instruction. In 1928, at the Rejaf Language Conference, a decision was taken to adopt English as the language of all official work, rejecting the pidgin Arabic which had up to then been the lingua franca of the South. In addition, Dinka, Shilluk, Nuer, Bari, Lotuko, and Zande were chosen as 'group' languages in which elementary vernacular textbooks would be written. This decision, together with the expressed policy that the aim of education in the South was 'to fit the ordinary individual to fill a useful part in his environment, with happiness to himself', was later to be criticized as embodying the 'Zoo' mentality.[9] Certainly the British were in no hurry to educate the Southern Sudanese, even after the mission schools were subsidized and inspected by the Government after 1926. This is shown by the fact that in 1948 there were exactly the same number of intermediate schools as there had been in 1928, namely three, that only seventeen Southerners attended secondary school, and that these were in Uganda.[10] How different the situation might have been today if only one good secondary school, such as King's College Budo in Uganda, had been producing students in the 1920s or 1930s!

Concerning local administration, the watchword of the British was 'indirect rule' in the South, as it was in other parts of British colonial Africa. But indirect rule required local chiefs, and finding a chief who could deal with and control his subjects in a manner approved by the Government was easier said than done. Some tribes had religious leaders rather than chiefs; others put forward a mere figurehead while the real chief remained in the background.

---

[8] For the boundaries of these mission spheres, see Said, op. cit., pp. 166 f.

[9] J. S. R. Duncan, *The Sudan* (Edinburgh, Blackwood, 1952), p. 217.

[10] L. Sanderson, 'Educational Development in the Southern Sudan 1900–48' *Sudan Notes and Records* (Vol. 43, 1962), p. 117.

Chiefs' courts, though eventually a success, were only with difficulty instituted.[11] Nevertheless the British were determined to make the policy of indirect rule work, and to preserve the purely African way of life of the Southern peoples. A logical consequence of this was that Arabic and Islamic influence would have to be excluded, and this line of thinking flowered in the famous Southern Policy.

SOUTHERN POLICY

Although the British had been gradually instituting what amounted to Southern Policy in a series of acts ranging from the substitution of Sunday for Friday as the day of rest in 1918[12] to the vigorous suppression of Northern attempts to raid the South for slaves under the very nose of the Government,[13] it was not until 1930 that Southern Policy was officially stated:

The Policy of the Government in the Southern Sudan is to build up a series of self-contained racial and tribal units with structure and organization based, to whatever extent the requirements of equity and good government permit, upon indigenous customs, traditional usage, and beliefs.[14]

What were the reasons that lay behind Southern Policy? If we dig deeply enough, they probably stem from a vague terror that Christians have had of Islam ever since the days of the Crusades. For example, in 1892 Lord Kitchener wrote the following memorandum on Uganda:

[11] R. O. Collins, 'The Sudan: Link to the North', in Diamond and Burke (eds.) *The Transformation of East Africa*, (New York, 1966), pp. 375-6.

[12] When the Belgians held the Lado Enclave, Sunday was the day of rest. But with the Condominium take-over in 1910, Friday was imposed. This caused a reaction among the missionaries, but the Government, fearing a rebellion among the Northern Muslim troops, waited until the troops had departed to restore Sunday. The Sudan Government publication, *Basic Facts about the Southern Provinces of the Sudan* (Khartoum, 1964), makes the significant error of stating that the change-over to Sunday occurred in 1938.

[13] See the account of such a raid by the Rizeigat near Raga in the Bahr el Ghazal in 1909, by R. C. Greenwood, *Sudan Notes and Records*.

[14] H. A. MacMichael (then Civil Secretary of the Sudan) in a secret memorandum on Southern Policy, now in the Sudan Government archives, quoted by Collins, in Diamond and Burke, op. cit., p. 378.

Unless the Christian powers hold their own in Africa, the Mohammedan Arabs will, I believe, step in, and in the centre of the continent will form a base from which they will be able to drive back all civilizing influences to the coast, and the country will then be given up to slavery and misrule as is the case in the Sudan at present.[15]

The fear that the centre of Africa might revert to Muslim rule was not entirely without foundation in the early years in the South—the Mahdists had attempted to rise in 1903 and 1908 and had been suppressed. This was, in fact, one of the reasons that led to the formation of the Equatorial Corps. But a reason of much more importance for the formation of the Southern Policy was the following. If the South was to be governed effectively, Southern confidence was needed. This confidence could not be won if Southerners' suspicion of a return to Mahdiya was fostered by the presence of too many *jallaba* (Arab traders) in the South. Memories of the slave trade were fresh, and, as mentioned above, slavery even continued for some years concurrently with the process of pacification in the South. Thus, as late as 1947, it was written:

Organized raiding continued as long as adjacent parts of the South were unadministered and therefore unprotected. In the late twenties, an extensive trade in slaves from Ethiopia was unmasked and even today there are occasional kidnappings and the victims are hurried into the hands of the desert nomads of the North.[16]

Probably the real reason for the introduction of Southern Policy, however, was that it was dictated by the thorough-going implementation of indirect rule. MacMichael and others saw that indirect rule required the Africanization of many aspects of life in the South. But, as Collins remarks:

In order to encourage indigenous, African customs in the South, all Northern Sudanese, Muslim, Arab influences were to be eradicated, for African traditions, already weakened by a

---

[15] Quoted by Collins, in Diamond and Burke, op. cit., p. 378.
[16] *The Sudan: A Record of Progress* (published by the Sudan Government, 1947).

century of chaos, could hardly hope to flourish in the face of the dynamic and expansive culture of the Northern Sudan.[17]

These were the reasons for the introduction of Southern Policy. It is only fair, however, to point out that not every writer on the Sudan regarded them as good ones, particularly the slave trade argument:

It was absurd to suggest that a trade which had flourished at a time when administrative control was either weak or totally absent could revive under the strong and honest rule established by the Condominium. Neither was it reasonable to assume that every Northern merchant in the South would be an unscrupulous shark, or that the Southerners would be so lacking in native wit as to be unable to deal with them.[18]

What did Southern Policy amount to in practice? First, all Northern administrative staff were transferred out of the Southern provinces, and the trading permits of Northerners withdrawn. In the western Bahr el Ghazal, where there were Arab immigrants from Darfur and Northern Nigeria, large-scale resettlement took place, and a no-man's land was created between South and North. Secondly, every administrator was instructed to speak the language of the people of his district, or, at second best, English, but never Arabic. He was to acquaint himself as closely as possible with local customs and beliefs. Thirdly, the wearing of Arabic dress and the use of Arabic names by Southerners were discouraged. These measures had their desired result— the Africanization of the South. But there were other less desirable effects. An unhappy D.C. wrote in 1941 that 'perhaps the most disappointing aspect of the working of Southern Policy is the failure to produce in ten years any Southern staff trained for executive work'.[19] Nor was it even clear that Southerners were being encouraged to seek jobs in the administration. Not until 1942 was the first Southerner, Mr. Stanislaus Paysama, allowed to sit for the Civil (now

[17] Collins, in Diamond and Burke, op. cit., p. 381.
[18] P. M. Holt, *A Modern History of the Sudan* (London, Weidenfeld and Nicholson, 1961), p. 150.
[19] Quoted by Collins, in Diamond and Burke, op. cit., p. 385.

Public) Service Examination. The next man was selected
for the exams in 1944, two in 1946, and a larger batch of
twelve sat in 1948. Since all these hand-picked candidates
passed the exams, it is difficult to understand why progress
towards localizing the staff was so gradual.

Shortly after the end of the war in 1945, Southern Policy
had progressed sufficiently far for the British to begin talk of
separating the Southern provinces from the North altogether,
and joining them up with East Africa. This was advocated
in a pamphlet issued by the Fabian Colonial Bureau in 1945,
entitled *The Sudan—the Road Ahead*, and in 1947 the Sudan
Government stated in their official publication, referred to
above:

the northern Sudanese fear that the ultimate result may be to
split the country in half and even to attach the south or part of
the south to Uganda. The arguments whether such a course
would be to the ultimate advantage of the Southern Sudan or
to the rest of Africa are many on both sides and the whole
question might at some date form a proper subject for consideration by an international commission.[20]

However, not every administrator in the Sudan felt that
it was desirable to separate the South from the North. The
following arguments for the other side, collected by K. D. D.
Henderson, were supported by many at the time:[21]

1. The boundary would be difficult to define satisfactorily.

2. The North on its own would find it difficult to avoid
being absorbed by Egypt.

3. There was African blood in every Northern tribe.

4. The South could supplement the Northern economy
with tropical products, which Uganda already had in
abundance.

5. If the South, while remaining essentially Southern,
could yet become an integral part of an independent Sudan,
it could help to bridge the inevitable gulf between Muslim
and non-Muslim, Asian and African, black and brown, in
the Africa of the future.

[20] *The Sudan: A Record of Progress.*
[21] K. D. D. Henderson, *Sudan Republic* (London, Benn, 1965), p. 164.

Still, in 1945 the prevailing official view was to be found in the Governor-General's restatement of Southern Policy:

The approved policy is 'to act upon the fact that the people of the Southern Sudan are distinctly African and Negroid, and that our obvious duty to them is therefore to push ahead as fast as we can with their economic and educational development on African and Negroid lines, and not upon the Middle Eastern and Arab lines of progress which are suitable for the Northern Sudan. It is only by economic and educational development that these people can be equipped to stand up for themselves in the future, whether their future lot be eventually cast with the Northern Sudan or with East Africa (or partly with each).'[22]

This view did not, however, prevail much longer, for in 1946 the whole situation changed radically.

THE REVERSAL OF SOUTHERN POLICY

By 1946, the Government began to feel Northern political pressure which had started with the emergence of the Graduates' Congress in the late 1930s. Since Egyptian politicians such as Sa'ad Zaghlul as early as 1924 had openly claimed the Sudan as their legal possession, and since in 1946 Arab nationalism in the Middle East was reaching new heights, the most sensible choice open to the British seemed to be to proceed cautiously in guiding the Sudan to independence, while retaining their base at the Suez Canal. Northern politicians urged the transformation of their Advisory Council, which was set up in 1944, into a legislative body which would be representative of the whole Sudan, including the South. To advise him on this matter the Governor-General appointed a special Sudan Administrative Conference which began its meetings in April 1946, sending one of its sub-committees on a lightening tour of the South. The sub-committee flew to Juba, and after only a few days returned to Khartoum urging the fusion of the South with the North. The Civil Secretary, J. W. Robertson, after approaching the East African authorities and finding that they were

[22] Khartoum Secret Despatch, 4 August 1945, quoted by Collins, in Diamond and Burke, op. cit., pp. 386–7.

unenthusiastic about either uniting with the Southern Sudan or developing communications with it, came to agree with this line of thinking, and in a letter to the Provincial Governors of 16 December 1946 announced the official abandonment of Southern Policy. In a paragraph, which should be compared with the Secret Despatch of 4 August 1945, he wrote:

The policy of the Sudan Government regarding the Southern Sudan is to act upon the facts that the peoples of the Southern Sudan are distinctively African and Negroid, but that geography and economics combine (so far as can be foreseen at the present time) to render them inextricably bound for future development to the middle-eastern and arabicized Northern Sudan; and therefore to ensure that they shall, by educational and economic development, be equipped to stand up for themselves in the future as socially and economically the equals of their partners of the Northern Sudan in the Sudan of the future.[23]

Reaction to this despatch was favourable, but with qualifications. The Deputy-Governor of Bahr el Ghazal, T. R. H. Owen, wrote of the proposed policy as follows:

I believe it to be the wisest and the rightest course, and one which I can follow loyally.
But that does not prevent certain misgivings. These misgivings are founded upon a knowledge of the shortcomings of the Northern Sudanese. That they could run Omdurman I believe. That they will soon be fit to govern the Rizeigat and the Hadendowa is possible. That they will in the next two decades be fit to be entrusted with the Zande and the Dinka is not even thinkable.[24]

When, however, the question of Southern participation in an All-Sudan Legislative Assembly was approved by the Sudan Administrative Conference in January 1947, opposition among the administrators in the South became more vocal. At this conference, the South was represented only by her two British Governors (Bahr el Ghazal being from 1940 to 1948 under Equatoria Province). In a letter to the

[23] For the full text of the letter, see Said, op. cit., pp. 162 f.
[24] Owen's full letter is in Said, op. cit., pp. 40 f.

Civil Secretary of March 1947, Owen and several others urged that since no effort had yet been made to obtain the opinion of leading Southerners on their own future, the Government should convene a separate administrative conference for the Southern Sudan. They made it clear, however, that their proposed conference was to take it for granted that 'the Sudan remains one country', and only to concern itself with laying down a policy of political development that would enable Southerners to take their place as equals of the North. Since this did not contradict the stand in Khartoum, the Civil Secretary readily accepted the proposal, and the conference opened in Juba on 12 June 1947.

THE JUBA CONFERENCE

The Juba Conference was composed of fifteen Southerners, chosen by the Governors of the Southern Provinces, six British officials, and six Northerners. It was presided over by the Civil Secretary, whose opening speech left no alternative for the South but union with the Arab North. He said: 'It has begun to be clear, I think, that the Southern Sudan, by its history and by the accidents of geography, river transport, and so on, must turn more to the North rather than to Uganda or the Congo.'[25]

The outcome of the Conference was certainly what the Government of the day had decided upon in 1946. Southerners tried to insist on speedy development of the South before the question of their participation in a joint legislative assembly with Northerners could be considered. But this view would not be tolerated by the Chairman. When the Chairman asked whether anyone present had any objections to the unity of the Sudan, Mohammed Saleh el Shingetti complained that this was outside the meeting's terms of reference. But Chief Lapponya pointed out that the principle of unity could only be decided later, when the Southerners were grown up, by which time they would be in a position to decide whether to join the North or go to the Belgian Congo or Uganda. To this, the Chairman explained that

[25] Proceedings of the Juba Conference, reprinted in full in Said, op. cit., pp. 46–71.

'people could not get up and go where they liked just like that'.

Meanwhile, every recess or adjournment was marked by threats, blackmail, and bribery from the Northern side to the Southerners. This being the very first time they had been invited by the Government to express their opinion about the future of their country, it is not even certain whether the Southern representatives were really confident that their views would be given any consideration. After all, they had hitherto only taken orders from the British administrators whose direct assistants were Northerners, and whatever the Chairman and a man like Judge Shingetti said appeared to many of them to be a correction of their views—an impression which both the British and the Northerners deliberately created and exploited. For instance, James Tambura changed his mind overnight, and confessed 'that Judge Shingetti had said that if they did not do so they would have no say in the future Government of the Sudan'. As one follows the development of Southern thought in the proceedings of the Conference, it becomes very clear from the class of people who began the change that they were enticed into thinking that the existing differences in salaries between the South and the North would be automatically corrected if they agreed to work together with the North. But perhaps what really helped to allay Southern fears of Northern domination was the Chairman's explanation 'that in any case according to the report of the Administrative Conference, all laws made by the Legislative Assembly would be referred to the Governor General for his comments'. Thus satisfied that British protection would not be removed altogether, and for the reasons outlined above, Southern delegates—with the exception of a few—accepted the idea of participating in a joint legislative assembly in Khartoum.

Two months later, the Civil Secretary wrote to the Southern Governors saying:

At the 559th meeting of His Excellency the Governor General's Council, the report of the Sudan Administrative Conference was submitted and the Council passed the following resolutions regarding the Southern Sudan:

'That the proposal that the Legislative Assembly should be representative of the whole Sudan and that its scope should not be limited to the Northern Sudan be accepted, but that safeguards be introduced which will ensure the healthy and steady development of the Southern peoples. . . .'

In my opinion, the South must be administered as an integral part of a united Sudan . . . it must be pointed out that progress in the South is dependent upon the Northern taxpayer and it is surely not unjust that if the Northern Sudan is paying some £900,000 in 1947 to make up the deficit on Southern revenue, it should have some say in how this money is being spent.[26]

For the British, it was a matter of prestige to crystallize their policy in the South in a form that could be publicly explained and supported. The reversal of Southern Policy was effected virtually overnight.

There is very little evidence, if any, to show that the Arabs of the Northern Sudan put up so much struggle for unity with the Africans of the South purely for its own sake. First of all, Northerners, encouraged by Egypt, wanted independence. Likening the separation of the South to the policy of 'divide and rule', they thought it would hasten the pace to independence if they made noise about unity. Secondly, the few projects that were started in the South made it imperative for Northerners to be employed in the Southern development schemes, and in fact many of them demanded employment in the South. They thought the only way to ensure such employment and to retain Northern salary scales was to merge the two regions. Thirdly, the South was, and still is, a potential source of wealth which Northerners had no wish to lose.[27] Fourthly, the lower type of Northern merchants (the *jallabas*) operated very profitably in the South, and Northerners could therefore not afford to lose such a market. Fifthly, if the South broke away, it was almost certain that Egypt would absorb the North. This is even more of a possibility now with the awakening of indigenous Africans in the Northern provinces who might

[26] Civil Secretary's Office, 21 August 1947, CS/1.A.9/2.
[27] On this subject, see Mekki Abbas, *The Sudan Question* (London, 1952), p. 182.

wish to join the South, and leave the North as a purely Arab, but helpless state. Even if Egypt did not use force, Northerners believe that the creation of a separate state in the South that might not be very friendly with them might drive them into a voluntary but undesirable union with Egypt. Sixthly, it is a matter of prestige to be able to keep boasting about their position of being a bridge between the Arab and the African worlds. Seventhly, there was the element of religious fervour in spreading Islam. Finally, power thirst and the desire to dominate a race cannot be altogether dismissed as being out of the question. All these factors put together gave the North that desperate incentive to keep the South; an incentive which has always proved to be invidious to the Southerners.

THE SUDAN UNDER THE LEGISLATIVE ASSEMBLY, 1948–53

Preparations for the eventual transfer of legislative powers to the Sudanese people were indeed rapid and deserve appreciation. Acting upon their own stated policy of preparing Southerners for their responsibilities as the equals of Northerners, and to allay Southern fears of Northern domination, the Zande Scheme was started in 1947 under the management of the Equatoria Projects Board to grow cotton and produce cloth in Yambio district. Sawmills were opened at Katire, Gilo, and Loka West; all-weather roads were constructed to link principal towns of the Southern Sudan; and trading licences were given to any Southerner or Northerner who fulfilled the basic commercial requirements. Restrictions on movement between the two parts of the country were relaxed. 'But, as in so many colonial areas of the world, the British in the Southern Sudan began with too little too late.'[28]

The years 1948–50 marked a momentous change in educational policy in the South. Subventions to mission schools were increased, and in 1948 the first secondary school was opened at Atar, in Upper Nile, and transferred in 1949 to Rumbek in Bahr el Ghazal. The custom of sending candidates for higher education to Makerere

[28] Collins, in Diamond and Burke, op. cit., p. 392.

College in Uganda was discontinued and Gordon College in Khartoum was used instead. But the really momentous change was the introduction of Arabic in 1950 as an academic subject in all schools above the elementary level, with a view eventually to making it the medium of instruction. This was duly accomplished in 1957, when all mission schools in the South were taken over by the Government, and all private schools (which are still common in the North) prohibited.

When the Legislative Assembly Ordinance (1948) was drafted, the Legal Secretary omitted the safeguards for the South referred to above on the grounds that since all legislation was subject to the Governor-General's veto, nothing adversely affecting the South would be approved at the palace. The Legal Secretary further argued that since Northern and Egyptian opinion would capitalize on the inclusion of such safeguards, it was safe from the British point of view to rely on the Governor-General's veto. This did not prove to be altogether correct.

The Legislative Assembly was opened on 15 December 1948 with thirteen nominated members from the South, seventy-six from the North, and six British. This was in complete disregard for the proposals put forward at the Juba Conference of June 1947 which said there should be '15 or more' Southern members drawn from Provincial Councils which would start to operate before the Legislative Assembly. External political events, no doubt, made the Governor-General reticent to use his veto at a time when the Condominium partnership was badly strained. In any case, if he had used the veto, it would have been ineffective without machinery through which he could assess Southern feelings. This machinery, I think, should have been in the form of the proposed Provincial Councils, since decisions in the Legislative Assembly were carried by simple majority, and there were only thirteen Southerners out of ninety-five members. It was, in fact, an obvious embarrassment for the Governor-General to veto legislation which had passed through the Legislative Assembly under the noses of Southern members as adversely affecting the Southern Sudan.

In the Legislative Assembly, the Southern members began on much the same note as did the delegates to the Juba Conference the year before. They pressed for speedy development, and dismissed any idea of self-government for the Sudan unless their proposals for such a speedy development were carried out. In the South, during the Council's recess, Southern members were presented with reports on the Northern scornful attitude towards Southerners, which had already began to produce sharp social and political frictions between the two groups as a result of the post-1947 influx of Northerners into the South. In many places, angry Southerners told these members to inform the Government that they preferred to join East Africa, but, as 'people could not get up and go where they like just like that', the members advised against it. They suggested instead that they would no longer stick to a speedy development programme only, but would, in addition, request that Southerners be allowed to run their own local affairs. I can vividly recall the rousing cheers given to Mr. Benjamin Lwöki in Loka in 1949 when he mentioned this. To the ordinary Southerner, running his own affairs automatically meant the exclusion of the Northern merchant who not only insults every Southerner as *abeed* (slave), but also offers a great deal of bad advice to the Northern administrator on the situation in the South. By 1950, Southerners in the Legislative Assembly were very definite on their demand for a federal status within one Sudan.

On 26 March 1951, a Constitution Commission was appointed to advise the Governor-General on steps to be taken for granting self-government. Mr. Buth Diu, who represented the South, called for a federal constitution. The Northern members of the Commission persistently rejected all his proposals. He walked out of a meeting, and when Northerners proved to be intransigent on his views, he finally withdrew from the Commission, thus leaving Northerners and some British officials to determine the future of the South in the context of a united Sudan. Pointing out the dangers of the Southern withdrawal from the Commission, the British officials on the Commission succeeded in including safeguards in the proposals which aimed at providing the South with a status similar to that of Northern Ireland in the United Kingdom. The Governor-General was also given wide legislative powers to afford protection over all the backward areas of the Sudan—including the South. The Commission's work was approved by the Legislative Assembly, and had the force of law until 1953.

The year 1951 saw the birth of the Southern Sudanese political movement. The founders of this movement were three men: Abdel Rahman Sule (a muslim, known for ever after to members of the movement as 'the Patron'), Stanislaus Paysama, and Buth Diu. In 1953, after Southerners were excluded from the Egyptian agreement on the grounds that they had no political party, the movement was officially registered as the Southern Party, and in 1954 changed its name to the Liberal Party. This party remained the sole representative of Southern aspirations and hopes until the dissolution of all political parties in 1958.

SELF-GOVERNMENT AND THE TRANSITION TO INDEPENDENCE, 1953–5

On 12 February 1953, an Anglo-Egyptian Agreement was signed granting self-government to the Sudan. The pace with which the Northern Arabs and the Egyptians achieved their aims at the conferences preceding this Agreement, and the exclusion of Southerners from them, clearly indicate that the underlying motive of the British was to induce the Egyptians to forget the Suez Canal question. They thought Egyptian demands for British evacuation of the Canal base would become secondary to their ambitions in the Sudan, and Sir Ralph Stevenson, the British Ambassador to Egypt, representing the British Government, was 'glad that the signing of this agreement will inaugurate a new era between Egypt and Great Britain'.[29] It never did. General Muhammad Neguib, Egypt's Prime Minister, attached so much urgency to the Suez question that he wanted to seize the opportunity to discuss it immediately. But Sir Ralph again hoped that 'this Agreement will prove a good augury for the next

[29] *The Anglo-Egyptian Agreement* (Cairo, February 1953).

round',[30] thus evading the idea of discussing the Canal base there and then.

The Anglo-Egyptian Agreement which had excluded Southerners from the Conference annulled Article 100 of the Self-Government Statute, which had been entrenched by the Constitution Commission and approved by the Legislative Assembly in 1951 to provide safeguards for the South. Instead, a provision was made in the Self-Government Statute giving the South at least two ministerial posts. If there were any Southerners blind to Northern intentions to dominate the South, this blindness was cured after the Agreement. Feelings against the North became extremely bitter and tensions rose very high. Many Southerners also began to lose faith in the British, feeling that they were all out to hand them to the Arabs for various reasons. Southerners therefore began to rely more on direct methods for the attainment of their ends than to pin any hopes on the Government. Mr. Buth Diu, who was then Secretary General of the Liberal Party, protested against the Agreement to the United Nations Organisation. Southern political consciousness, owing its existence to a series of mistakes on the part of the Government and Northern political parties was now too well crystallized to be either ignored or suppressed.

Nevertheless, Southerners participated in the October 1953 elections. The South was granted twenty-two out of ninety-seven seats. Despite this obvious Southern minority, Northern administrators in the South, who always acted as representatives of various Northern political parties, did their best to reduce effective representation by disqualifying candidates who opposed Northern policies and tried to promote Southern interests. An example of this case was Mr. Cipriano Koryang who was disqualified as being 28 in 1953 and therefore under age. In 1958 he was disqualified for the same reason, thus allowing his Northern opponent to be elected unopposed. The prescribed age was 30.

During the election campaign in the South, the pro-Egyptian National Unionist Party (N.U.P.) made every effort to woo Southern voters. The Egyptian Special

[30] Ibid.

Ministers for Sudan Affairs, Major Salah Salim, toured the South addressing public meetings, and promised the Southerners forty posts as Governor, D.C., and A.D.C. when the British left. At these meetings the backwardness of the South and the nakedness of some tribes were the main theme, and were blamed on the British. At Rumbek Major Salim tried to prove that the Egyptians had historical and blood relations with the Dinka tribe. Attributing the difference in the colour of his skin to the climate, he at one time took off his shirt and joined a Dinka dance. But he could not take off his pair of shorts and shoes because, while he had become used to them, the British had deprived his 'brothers in the South' of them. Southerners, he said, would soon realize how elementary these things were when they were united with Egypt.

Despite Major Salim's efforts, the N.U.P. won only six of the Southern seats, the remaining sixteen being won by the Southern Party. But in the Sudan as a whole the elections brought an overwhelming majority for the N.U.P. The party chairman, Ismail el Azhari, therefore formed the Government and became the Sudan's first Prime Minister. Azhari's first major action was the appointment of a Sudanization Committee on 20 February 1954. At the end of July, the Committee reported that there were 800 posts to be Sudanized. A Public Service Commission—consisting entirely of Northerners—was set up to effect recruitment and appointment to these posts. When Sudanization was complete, only four junior posts of Assistant District Commissioner and two of *Mamur* were given to the South. There was no excuse for this because a pro-Egyptian clerk at Juba Provincial Headquarters was promoted and transferred to the North as a Deputy Governor and later as Governor Designate, while his younger Southern assistant, Mr. James Tambura, was said to be approaching the 'age of retirement'. There is no doubt that the results of Sudanization added more fuel to the already deteriorating relations between the South and the North. This may be best expressed in the words of Mr. Gregory Deng Kir, a Southern merchant, who wrote to the Southern Members of Parliament as follows:

D

'The results of Sudanization have come out with a very disappointing result, i.e. four Assistant District Commissioners, Well as it appears, it means our fellow Northerners want to colonize us for another hundred years.'[31]

Southern fears and suspicions reached their climax. At this juncture Southern leaders, irrespective of party, decided to rally the masses and intellectuals so as to face the North as a united front in presenting their demands to Parliament.

A Liberal Party Conference was therefore convened in Juba in October 1954. The injustices of the Public Service Commission occupied much of the debates, and a resolution was unanimously passed demanding federal status for the South, and calling upon Southerners, irrespective of their party, 'to be ready for sacrifices'. The Southern leaders' efforts met with so much success that an observer had this to say:

The demand for federation had, however, spread widely beyond the small educated elite to the chiefs, village headmen, and their followers, since it reflected a general Southern—Black African— fear of the Arab Northern domination.[32]

At the beginning of 1955 a delegation of the N.U.P., headed by the Prime Minister, visited the Southern Sudan in an attempt to undo the Liberal Party's work and weaken any further efforts by the Southern leaders. 'They were booed and ill-received everywhere.' In order to gain an audience, and to counteract the obvious success of the Liberal Party in rallying the masses behind them, Mr. Azhari promised a rise in the salaries of clerks, police, and prison warders. 'This was regarded by Southerners as a bribe and in any case created discontent as it did not include Article III Clerical Category, who form the majority of the clerks in the South, despite the recommendations of the Governors that these should be included.'[33]

---

[31] Quoted in the *Report of the Commission of Enquiry into the Disturbances in the Southern Sudan during August 1955* (Khartoum, 1956), p. 144.

[32] Ronald Segal *Political Africa: A Who's Who of Personalities and Parties* (London, Stevens, 1961), p. 448.

[33] *Report of the Commission of Enquiry . . . August 1955*, op. cit., p. 21.

In pursuance of the resolutions of their conference of October 1954 in Juba, the Liberal Party leaders called upon all Southern Members of Parliament, regardless of party, to form a Southern Bloc to pursue Southern demands. Responding to this appeal, the Southern members of the N.U.P. who were ministers in Azhari's Government sharply disagreed with him on his handling of Southern affairs. One of them subsequently resigned, and the other was dismissed from the cabinet. They joined the Liberal Party, which decided to hold another conference in June 1955 in Juba in order to consolidate its plans within a Southern Bloc.

Because invitations were sent even to Southern parliamentary members in the N.U.P., the government attempted to frustrate this conference, and for this purpose it appears a hint was sent from a government source to some politically minded administrators in Equatoria for telegrams to be sent to Khartoum deprecating the aims of the Juba Conference, and supporting the government. The District Commissioner Yambio, and the Assistant District Commissioner Yambio, whereupon toured their district to obtain from chiefs signatures supporting the government. All forms of pressure was used to obtain their consent, trickery not excluded.[34]

It is needless to point out that reactions thus obtained from Southern chiefs under duress were given much publicity by the Government radio at Omdurman.

The Egyptian *coup d'état* of July 1952 which led to King Farouk's abdication of the throne, bringing General Mohammed Neguib to power, eventually had its repercussions on Sudanese politics. On 2 November 1952, General Neguib—himself half Sudanese—made a declaration renouncing any Egyptian claim over the Sudan and recognizing the Sudanese right to self-determination (thus paving the way for the 12 February 1953 Agreement). Neguib's renunciation of the Egyptian claim also encouraged the N.U.P. eventually to abandon their slogan of 'unity with Egypt' in a party resolution passed on 31 March 1955. It

[34] Ibid., p. 87.

was the only sensible thing to do, since the difficulties of achieving such a union were obvious. It was also the only way the N.U.P. could cling to power.

On 16 August 1955 Parliament unanimously adopted a resolution to the effect that since Sudanization had been completed, 'arrangement for self-determination should be put in motion forthwith'. In his statement, Mr. Azhari said the question of a link with Egypt would now be subject to a plebiscite. One is tempted to suspect that this was calculated to reduce the gap between the N.U.P. and the Umma Party so as to face the developing situation in the South as a united front. This is virtually confirmed by events leading to the Southern uprising. Whatever was the case, differences between these Arab parties were so reduced that a National Coalition Government was later formed.

THE SOUTHERN UPRISING OF AUGUST 1955

While everything appeared to be running smoothly in Parliament, suspicious circumstances were developing in the South. No doubt history played a great part in the Southern uprising, and Northerners always behaved as a constant reminder of the past by referring to Southerners as *abeed*. The sudden change from the paternal attitude of the British administrators to the tough, scornful Arab rulers destroyed any vestiges of confidence that some Southerners might have had in Northerners. Moreover, many Southerners who had served together with Northerners in the Second World War, and those who had been to the North, knew too well the Arabs' weaknesses to accept them as masters. With the growing momentum of Southern political aspirations, Northerners generally felt that they would ultimately have to resort to the use of force.

The proximate causes of the uprising were therefore the Arabs themselves. Public administrators were a carefully selected group of party emissaries who used their offices as propaganda centres for promoting party interests. Southern generosity and sociability were always mistaken for ingenuousness, thus encouraging the most unscrupulous bureaucracy. When it was realized that Southerners were not too simple to pursue their political demands, these administrators, who had by now lost the confidence of all the people, requested that Northern troops be stationed in the South in case of any disloyalty by the Southern Corps. Their fears had been aroused in July when 300 Southern workers on the Zande Scheme demonstrated against their sudden dismissal and were shot down by the army and police. But the *Kaid* (Officer Commanding Sudan Army) turned down the request for troops because he genuinely thought that there was no cause for suspicion, and such action might only risk creating unnecessary ill-feeling among the natives. Nevertheless, by manipulating tension among the Southerners themselves, the Arab administration successfully created conditions which conformed to their wishes to move Northern troops to the South—the 'discovery' on 7 August 1955 of an alleged conspiracy to mutiny in the Southern Corps. Some 500 Northern troops were subsequently flown to Juba. As the *Kaid* had predicted, this was widely interpreted in the South—by both Northerners and Southerners, each in their own way to their own satisfaction—as the beginning of an armed invasion and occupation of the South. The entire Southern Corps, starting with No. 2 Company in Torit, was to be sent to the North and be broken up. The most critical meeting was held at the Muderia (provincial headquarters) at Juba on 17 August 1955. By then it was clear that No. 2 Company would very likely refuse to obey orders. Various suggestions were made, among them that all the ammunition at Torit should be exploded by Northern Officers in Torit. These suggestions were ruled out by the Commanding Officer as he thought that '*such an action would provoke troops to start something even if they had not thought of it, and in any case, he was confident that the Company would obey orders*'(authors italics).'[35]

Determined to have their demands for the disbandment of the Southern Corps fulfilled, the administration persisted against the O.C.'s wishes, and the decision was finally

[35] *Report of the Commission of Enquiry . . . August 1955*, op cit., pp. 108–9. Note the inconsistency of the O.C.'s remarks with the alleged discovery of a conspiracy to mutiny ten days earlier.

reached that No. 2 Company must, for the prestige and dignity of the army, proceed to Khartoum.

Just prior to departure, Yusbashi (Captain) Salah issued a threat to the Company to the effect that there were already 'five hundred troops in Juba who will come and kill you'. In case of any disobedience or mutiny, 'you must remember', he said, 'that there are twelve thousand troops in Khartoum who will come and kill you'.[36]

Under these circumstances, No. 2 Company naturally disobeyed orders to go to Khartoum. The prestige of the army as well as the administration in Equatoria had been already lost, and the decision not to alter previous orders and not to make alternative plans shows a reckless disregard for their feelings, especially when mounting political tension between the Arab North and the African South was common knowledge. This led to a mutiny of the entire Southern Corps. To the ordinary man, the die was cast to rid himself of Arab domination, and the 'mutiny' quickly developed into a popular uprising, varying only in intensity, throughout the Southern Sudan. Many Northerners as well as Southerners lost their lives during the uprising. Later, when the insurrection was over, a spirit of revenge dominated the trials of Southerners who had been implicated, except in cases where a show of justice was maintained to impress foreigners. Some of the survivors, like the D.C.s of Yambio and East Bank and the A.D.C. of Yambio, were appointed as judges in these trials. Having seen their previous political activities, can we not regard them as sitting as judges on their own cases? Life became very cheap, and people passed away daily in firing squads, from random shooting, torture in prisons, or in secret night arrests. It was in this atmosphere that independence resolutions were being hurried through Parliament. When certain implicating documents were produced which carried the names of some Southern politicians but did not bear any evidence of their being partners to the conspiracy, certain Southern M.P.s like Mr. Buth Diu decided to identify themselves with the Government party. Others simply cast their vote with the

[36] Ibid., pp. 107–8.

Government against their conscience in order to escape arrest and prosecution.

FIRST YEARS OF INDEPENDENCE

On 19 December 1955, amidst a reign of terror in the South, a resolution was passed to declare independence for the Sudan on 1 January 1956. To soften the remaining hard core of the Liberal Party, another resolution was unanimously passed to the effect that the House recommended that the Constituent Assembly (a body to be elected after independence with the dual capacity of constitutional body and parliament) should give Southern demands for federation 'full consideration'. Since this was the very first time Northerners had ever shown signs of recognition of their demands, the Southern M.P.s were led to believe in their sincerity. On 1 January 1956, the Self-Government Statute ceased to operate, and the transitional Constitution came into force. The Governor-General, who was also Commander-in-Chief of the Sudanese Armed Forces, was replaced by a five-man Supreme Commission, which included the Southerner Siricio Iro, and which elected a president in a monthly rotation from among its members. The Arabs were now in complete control of their own as well as of African destiny in the South. While Northerners feasted in celebration, Southerners retired to their houses, wondering what would befall them next, since the Arabs had been able to make a show of superiority under the Self-Government Statute even while there was still a British Governor-General. Reports from many places revealed that after the flag-raising ceremony, Northerners generally turned to Southern participants and told them that they were 'now going to be under their feet'. This saying became widespread in the South, and from the military régime to this day it has almost replaced the word *abeed*. In the process, the past has merely been translated into the present, for what difference is there between being an *abeed* and being *taht jesma* (literally, under shoes or feet)?

Having gone this far, a split between the pro-Egyptian hardcore of the N.U.P. and those who were in favour of an independent Sudan forced Azhari out of power. An Umma

Government was formed on 7 July 1956 in coalition with the People's Democratic Party (P.D.P.) and the Liberals. With regard to the South, it was more of a reshuffle than a real change in Government. The Umma not only followed in the footsteps of their predecessors, but openly showed their declared policy in the words of Mohammed Ahmed Mahgoub, who became Foreign Minister, that Africans could 'only understand the language of force'. There was, however, one good thing that this change from N.U.P. to Umma brought to the public. In accordance with the Commission of Enquiry Ordinance 1954, a Commission was appointed on 8 September 1955 by Azhari's Council of Ministers 'to inquire into, and report upon the recent disturbances in the Southern Sudan, and their underlying causes'. The frankness of the report shows very clearly how difficult it would have been to reveal the facts under the same Government which had caused the uprising. The report therefore appeared when the N.U.P. was in opposition, and they made every effort to destroy it. As the public rushed to bookshops and sales agents, they were usually told that the report was out of stock. Many urgent copies were printed without the map of the Southern Sudan in order to meet public demand. People wondered what was happening to the report. The fact was simple. The N.U.P. spent large sums of money purchasing stocks of the document for destruction lest the Umma should use it to gain prestige, and thus have the advantage over them in the forthcoming elections. The P.D.P. Minister of the Interior in the coalition, on the other hand, was determined to take advantage of the situation to build up his party's prestige.

Parliament was dissolved on 30 June 1957 in preparation for elections which took place from 27 February to 9 March 1958. Although the Arab administrators used their offices to suppress Southern candidates who supported Southern demands, they succeeded in only a very few cases. Twenty-five members from the forty-six Southern constituencies formed the Southern Bloc. Eleven members were uncommitted or independent, although one of the independents, the Rev. Fr. Saturnino Lohure, was elected by the Bloc as

Chairman of the Liberal Party Parliamentary Group. One Federalist member, Mr. Ezbon Mondiri, was imprisoned for seven years, apparently for his clear-cut pursuance of Southern demands. Southerners had hitherto demanded federal status without defining what type of federation they would settle for. Mr. Mondiri not only defined what kind, but drafted a constitution on U.S.A. lines for presentation to the Constituent Assembly. He also went a step farther by trying to rally Northern politicians from underdeveloped areas to support the Southern demand. In the North, the Umma Party gained sixty-three seats and formed another coalition with the P.D.P., who numbered twenty-seven. The N.U.P., with forty-five members, and one member of the Anti-Imperialist Front, together with the Southern members, sat in opposition. The total number of seats was 173.

This Parliament, which was also to sit as a Constituent Assembly, opened with difficulties for the South. To hasten the work of the Assembly, a forty-six-man Constitution Committee was set up in December 1956 to prepare a draft constitution. The three Southern members on the Committee pressed for a federal constitution, but by a democratic simple majority process, the forty-three Northern members simply went ahead drafting a unitary, Islamic Constitution. The three Southerners therefore withdrew from the Committee in December 1957, and when the draft was tabled before the Constituent Assembly for approval, the Southern Bloc naturally opposed it. Their proposal for a rectification of the draft to accommodate Southern views was rejected by the North as a bloc. In the most carefree and provocative manner, Mr. Mahgoub declared that they (the Arabs) had 'given the Southern claim for federation a very serious consideration, and found that it could not work in this country'. Due to such difficulties, Southern members walked out and decided to boycott all sittings connected with the draft constitution. After much persuasion and lobbying from the Northerners, Southern delegates returned to the Assembly only to explain their viewpoint and withdrew.

Outside the Constituent Assembly, Southern M.P.s spared no effort to lobby M.P.s from the relatively under-developed areas of the Sudan, promising them support for their demands in return. Consequently, the indigenous African population in the North began to demand measures of decentralization which would give them a right to run their local affairs. On 13 August 1958 the Beja tribal chiefs and their M.P.s invited the Prime Minister, Mr. Abdalla Khalil, and his cabinet to Port Sudan to present them with a demand for managing their local affairs. Upon his return to Khartoum, Mr. Khalil was presented with a similar demand by M.P.s from Kordofan and Darfur provinces. By September and October, it become abundantly clear that the indigenous African populations were going to rally support and press for a federal system in the Sudan so as to be less subjected to the Arab Government of Khartoum. At the same time, Azhari's N.U.P. appeared to be ready to throw in its lot with these movements, and was therefore regaining popularity. Furthermore, the coalition between the Umma and the P.D.P. was threatened by a dispute over the Umma Party's desire to make the Sudan an Islamic kingdom with Abdel Rahman el Mahdi its first monarch. In October the capital was swarming with demonstrations against the Government. All this, coupled with the Government's inability to save the country from its economic crisis, was bound to topple Khalil's Government. After making fruitless attempts to dissuade Southern M.P.s from pursuing their demands—sometimes using threats—the Umma Party handed over power to the army, who were becoming increasingly suspicious about their coalition with the P.D.P.

THE ARMY TAKE-OVER

By November 1958, the Government of Khalil badly needed a revolution in order to get its basic machinery going. The only alternative would have been to risk a general election, which would have undoubtedly have scraped clean all that remained in the treasury. Between the months of August and October, General Ibrahim Abboud made two political statements which alarmed many people who had hitherto completely dissociated the army from politics. The first statement dwelt much on the country's economic state, and the second combined the state of the economy with the 'integrity and sovereignty' of the country. The army, he said, would not stand by to allow the country to collapse and disintegrate. It was feared that any army take-over would affect the South very badly, and would in fact be calculated to prevent Southerners from making their demand for a federal constitution—a demand which was also quickly spreading in the North among the indigenous non-Arab tribes. A group of us therefore found our way into the house of Mr. Siricio Iro, the Liberal member of the Supreme Commission, in order to ascertain the reasons for Abboud's statements. He confessed that most of the Government's services were being paid out of money which had originally been borrowed from foreign countries for development schemes, and neither the beginning of these schemes nor the repayment of these loans was in sight. 'If nothing happens to change the situation, we shall not be able to pay for our services in the next month or two', he said. He then concluded by telling us that they had over 250,000 bales of cotton which the Umma Government was reluctant to sell because of a drop in world prices at a time when they had pledged to fetch good prices as part of their electoral programme. For these reasons, he thought Parliament would have to be suspended and a state of emergency declared in order to put matters right. He was aware that the Umma Party might want to hand over the Government to the army because General Abboud's second-in-command, General Abdel Wahab, who would most likely head such a Government, was an Umma member. General Abboud could then go on pension.

In any case, the army was blessed and given the go-ahead by Khalil's Government. Mr. Elia Lupe Baraba told me that he and his group were invited to Mr. Khalil's house on 15 November 1958 and asked to choose between forsaking their demands to form a coalition with Umma, and being silenced by a military government. They dismissed this as an idle threat. On 17 November 1958, the army seized power.

But it was not long before the Umma strong man, Ahmed Abdel Wahab, was removed by his colleagues from the army, thus depriving the Umma Party of its direct influence over the military junta. Two abortive *coups d'états* were attempted within the army in March and November 1959 which would have perhaps cleared the military government of its religious and traditional affiliations.

For the South, the military régime meant the silencing of any talk about federation. On arrival at Juba, the Southern M.P.s were summoned to the Governor's office where they were warned that the new régime would not tolerate politicians who uttered such evil words as federation. Wherever they were, the Government was going to keep an eye on politicians who might try to work against the unity of the country. Every enlightened[37] Southerner was classified as a politician and therefore a trouble-maker. If it were a matter of being silent, I sincerely believe that very few if any Southern politicians would have been troubled by the Government's threats. But the Government no doubt had a long prepared plan which had to be carried out whether conditions were favourable or not. All Southern ex-M.P.s and politicians were surrounded by informers who were in fact *agents provocateurs*. Arrests without charges, police searches, and imprisonment for fabricated charges were very common. No one could be certain of his neighbour.

In 1959, an ex-M.P., Dominic Muorwel, was arrested in Maridi as he was trying to leave the country with the intention of setting up a political movement in exile. Muorwel was reported to have been beaten so badly that he lay in hospital unable to move for eight months, as a result developing a fanatical hatred for Arabs.[38] He was sentenced to ten years imprisonment but released in September 1962.

In December 1960, a plot to carry out a mass arrest of Southern ex-M.P.s and politicians on Christmas eve was discovered, and a group of them including Father Saturnino and Joseph Oduho had to leave the country immediately.

[37] 'Enlightened' in the Southern Sudan ranged from being educated to merely being neatly dressed or failing to behave as an inferior to Northerners.
[38] *Weekly News* (Nairobi), 8 January 1965, p. 18.

It was, however, an alternative which many of them had contemplated for some time, since not only oppression but corruption was rapidly spreading in the South. In fact, if ever there was a time when corruption was most connived at, it was during the military régime, because it was a crime to point out any mistakes or false moves. The Southern M.P.s and others who left the country therefore decided to set up an organization in exile which would act as a mouthpiece for the Southern case.

In February 1962 three Southern political refugees, who were in Leopoldville (now Kinshasa) founded an organization with the rather unwieldy name of the Sudan African Closed Districts National Union (S.A.C.D.N.U.). The three were Father Saturnino and Joseph Oduho, mentioned above, and William Deng, who abandoned his service with the Sudan Government as A.D.C. of Kapoeta to join the others in exile. The officers of the group were Oduho (President), Marko Rume (Vice-President, replaced late in 1963 by Dominic Muorwel after his release from prison), Deng (Secretary-General), and Aggrey Jaden (Deputy Secretary-General). In 1963 the name was changed to the Sudan African National Union (S.A.N.U.) and, after some shifting around, its headquarters were settled in Kampala.

It appears that the attempted arrest of the politicians in 1960 was calculated to behead the Southern movement, in order to facilitate a return to parliamentary life in the Sudan without any threats of federation. Although this was made impossible by the fleeing of the Southerners from the country, the Arabs never had the slightest sense of caution. The administrators became even more unscrupulous than before. Having imprisoned some Southern elite and placed the rest under close surveillance, Mr. Ali Baldo said in Juba:

We thank God that by virtue of the marvellous efforts of the Revolutionary Government, the country will remain forever united. You should turn a deaf ear to any evil talk which comes from politicians, as you well know what has become of them in the past few years and you certainly don't want bloodshed again in the South. You are aware that anybody who interferes with public peace and tranquility will be dealt with severely and at once. During the days of Parliament, the Southern Parliamentary members advocated a federal government for the South. Such ideas are gone with politicians.[39]

Most subsequent arrests were for alleged interference 'with public peace and tranquility'. Examples of such arrests are innumerable. I describe my own case in Chapter 3, and here will only mention a few which I witnessed. In 1962 a boy came into Yei town to sell his goat. An Arab merchant, Mustafa Yassin, called him into his shop and tried to bargain for a reduction of the price. When the boy proved to be stubborn, he was caught, tied up, and thrown into a military lorry by soldiers who happened to be shopping at that time. The goat was left for the merchant while the boy was carried away to be tortured in the military detention camp. An eye-witness who was tailoring in the shop at the time gave me a full account of the story, and while playing tennis with the D.C. I brought the case up for discussion. He told me that the boy had been heard mentioning the name of Kisanga who was an 'outlaw'. I tried in vain to ascertain in what context a person who was engaged in a bargain about a goat could utter that name.

In another case, a military convoy found a certain Southern trader standing by the roadside on his bicycle to let them pass. The officer ordered the convoy to stop, the man's pockets were searched, all his money taken, and he was taken to the military detention camp for having an East African note of 20 shillings. I persuaded the police officer to intervene and let the police take up the case, but the army argued that only 'outlaws' could possess foreign money and, since it was their duty to eradicate them, they could not allow the police to interfere. This was, of course to conceal the soldiers' theft of the man's money. Many people lost their lives this way, either through torturing or by being shot in cold blood.

In October 1962, all Southern schools went on strike on hearing of preparations being made for guerilla warfare. The students and pupils knew the Arab mentality very well, and were aware that if a single Arab was killed, they would

[39] *Morning News* (Khartoum), 29 March 1961.

turn to places like the schools for vengeance. Many students were inhumanely flogged and imprisoned. Since then, Southern schools have never functioned normally, and in 1964 all schools were closed.

The guerilla warfare mentioned above did in fact break out in at least three attacks by Southerners during Abboud's régime. The first and second of these took place on 9 and 19 September 1963, respectively, when the police posts at Pachola (near the Ethiopian border) and Kajo Kaji were over-run and several Northern policemen killed. The third occurred on 11 January 1964, where a much larger force attempted to capture the town of Wau. They almost succeeded, but were finally driven off. During 1963 the Southern Freedom Fighters had organized themselves under the name 'Anya-Nya', which in the Madi language means 'snake poison'.[40] The Anya-Nya, which contains a large number of the old Equatoria Corps who mutinied in 1955, have continued to be an active force in the Southern Sudan up to the present day.

Although the task set by the military Government was to obliterate differences between the Arab North and the African South, the force with which they had tried to impose this 'solution' only sparked off the long smouldering resentment of Arab domination into armed rebellion. As the army tried to meet force with force, they turned wild on the civil population, thus driving thousands of people out of the country. Despite the fact that many of these refugees were able to make the world aware of what was going on in the Sudan, the Arab Government thought the best way to keep the world ignorant was to implicate the missionaries and expel them, and this was done under the Minister of the Interior's orders on 27 February 1964. On the contrary, the Southern case became so well known that the shame of it brought down the military junta.

THE FALL OF ABBOUD AND THE CARETAKER GOVERNMENT

The fall of Abboud had its root causes in the Southern problem. Although resentment of the military régime had

[40] Literally, the venom of the Gabon Viper.

reached a climax in the North, events leading to its rapid downfall were precipitated by the shooting of a Khartoum University student when students insisted on being allowed to pursue discussions on the situation in the Southern Sudan to a conclusion. There were mixed motives for the deposition of Abboud. The political parties in the North had formed a 'United National Front' as early as 1960 in order to put pressure on the army to re-establish parliamentary democracy. Some more radical officers in the army conspired with some of the political parties, such as the Sudan Communist Party and the Professional Front, with the hope of gaining their confidence in order to establish what they called a 'socialist state'. Others simply reacted from a disturbed conscience or disgust for military rule, and wished to regain the popularity of the army by re-establishing a parliamentary régime. The rest were straightforward party supporters, and were automatically members of the 'United National Front'. These factors combined to bring about the fall of the military junta with a week's rioting by unarmed populace against the heavily armed military dictatorship.

No Southerner was under the illusion that the Caretaker Government was going to be any different from past or future Arab Governments with regard to its policy in the South. Just as the military junta had been installed in order to suppress African aspirations in the South, the Arabs deposed it in favour of a constitutionally impotent Caretaker Government so as to consolidate their position and speak with one voice against the South, thus gaining time and Northern public opinion in the interim period. Nevertheless, the need to pursue a solution to the problem in a diplomatic way prevailed in the minds of Southern leaders inside the country.

After Abboud's fall on 21 October 1964, an agreement was reached on 30 October between the 'United National Front' and representatives of the Armed Forces regarding the following:

(1) The liquidation of military rule and the formation of a care-taker government whose main responsibility is to pave the way for the election of a Constituent Assembly.

(2) The revival of freedoms such as the freedom of expression, freedom of the press, freedom of association, etc.

(3) Cancellation of all laws which restrict freedom and the lifting of the state of emergency *except in areas where security might be endangered* (author's italics).

(4) Safeguarding the independence of the judiciary.

(5) Safeguarding the independence of the University.

(6) The release of all political detainees and the release of all civilians sentenced to imprisonment for political reasons.

(7) That the care-taker government will be committed to a foreign policy which is against colonialism and military pacts.

(8) That a court of appeal will be formed consisting of a minimum number of five judges to whom the judicial and administrative powers of the Chief Justice will be transferred.

(9) That a committee shall be set up to enact laws which will be in keeping with our traditions.

But, of course the achievement of this task will be an absolute impossibility if the security situation in the Southern Provinces has not come back to normal.[41]

This qualification left no doubt in Southern minds about Arab intentions to perpetuate their domination by military means under the pretext of quelling a rebellion.

It was clear that a demand on the Southern nationals to surrender their arms to a government headed by a race who had caused them to take up these arms would meet with no favourable response. Having said that the Southern problem is 'the most urgent national issue of our time, and therefore must be tackled very quickly and energetically', and having admitted that 'force is no solution to this vital human problem which has so many facets, social, economic and cultural', Prime Minister Sir el Khatim el Khalifa's Caretaker Government appears to have been charged with the task of quietly moving more troops to the South. During the military régime, there were some 12,000 Arab troops occupying the South. The Caretaker Government, which was described as 'the people's government', could virtually rely on the police for maintaining law and order in the North. The rest of the troops were therefore almost all moved to the

---

[41] Prime Minister's speech, *Policy of the Caretaker Government on the South* (Ministry of Information and Labour Printing Press, 1964), pp. 1–3.

South—raising the number to about 18,000, nearly the entire Sudanese Army. Questioners were told that a possible Tshombe invasion was anticipated, and troops had to stand by. But this answer could not explain reinforcements to areas nearer to the Northern Sudan, such as Upper Nile Province and most part of Bahr el Ghazal Province.

THE ROUND TABLE CONFERENCE

The Caretaker Government created a situation for which Southerners should be grateful, that is, the Khartoum Round Table Conference on the South which gave some seven African countries (Algeria, Ghana, Kenya, Nigeria, Tanzania, Uganda, and the United Arab Republic) the chance to decide on where to throw their sympathy after hearing both sides. Another remarkable feature of the Caretaker Government was its admission that the Southern problem is due to obvious natural differences. Mr. Khalifa said:

The Government is determined to admit with courage and full understanding the failures of the past and face up to its difficulties. It also recognises fully the ethical and cultural difference between North and South which have been brought about largely through geographical and historical factors.[42]

Southern leaders in exile were, for some time, determined that the conference be held outside the Sudan. Their reasons were clear. There was the fear for their own safety. But, more important, the Khartoum Arab Government hung at the mercy of the mob. Power had been shifted from a few military officers under Abboud's direction into the streets of Northern towns, and it was feared that if the talks did not proceed according to the feelings of the mob, the Government could be brought down, and the talks would thus be jeopardized. Another reason was that if the talks were held outside the Sudan, the observers would automatically assume a certain advisory capacity in their efforts to guide the conference towards what might be the best solution. In Khartoum, on the other hand, they were in the embarrassing position of being guests of one of the contending sides.

[42] In his opening address to the Round Table Conference.

Outside the Sudan, no side would be subjected to public pressure because the atmosphere would be foreign to both. Finally, machinery to guarantee the implementation of any agreement reached could be easily devised, whereas in the Sudan, Northerners pinned all their hopes on being trusted as a sovereign state to implement the agreements.

Inside the country the position of the Southern leaders was somewhat different. On the re-establishment of civilian rule a group called the Southern Front was formed, composed mainly of Southern students and civil servants in Khartoum. Their president was Gordon Abiei, a lawyer. They nominated three cabinet ministers to the Caretaker Government, including the Minister of the Interior, Clement Mboro, a long-time administrator who had served under the British in the South and had taken part in the Juba Conference.[43] The Southern Front agreed with those in exile that the conference should be held outside the Sudan, and for virtually the same reasons. But later, when William Deng broke with his S.A.N.U. colleagues and went back into the Sudan prepared to offer federation as a solution (it is believed that the Southern Front wanted the North to offer it first, and negotiate from there), the Southern Front was threatened with isolation both by the Arab Government, who were prepared to negotiate with William Deng alone, and by the Southern masses, who would have considered it a sign of weakness for them to hand leadership to Mr. Deng, whose views were not acceptable. Thus, from the time Deng went to Khartoum in February 1965 up to the first week of March, the Southern Front had a busy time trying to convince S.A.N.U. to come into the Sudan to save the situation. They also thought such a move would overcome Arab suspicion that S.A.N.U.'s obstinacy might lead to more

[43] A tragic incident occurred on Sunday 6 December 1964 when Mboro was Minister of the Interior. He had been on a fact-finding tour of the South, and a large crowd of Southerners who had gathered at the Khartoum airport to await his arrival rioted when it was rumoured (incorrectly) that he had been delayed by foul play. They in turn ran into an even larger crowd of Northerners coming out of a football match and took refuge in the American Mission. The building was burned to the ground, and it is thought that many hundreds of Southerners perished. (See Henderson, op. cit., p. 211.) Since then, those Southerners who continue to live in Khartoum do so in some trepidation.

violence, and thus win their good-will to reduce the number of their troops in the South. The inflow of Arab troops to the South was more to safeguard the Northerners *vis à vis* Mr. Deng's position, and to build him up as a puppet Southern leader, than for the disarmament of the Southern Freedom Fighters. There is no doubt that Northern opinion would have welcomed a boycott of the conference by S.A.N.U. so that they could persuade William Deng to accept something less than federal status for the South, and since Southerners might cause violence on the grounds that he was not their leader, these troops would be ready to suppress them.

S.A.N.U. eventually decided to attend the conference on the condition that African observers were invited from ruling parties, not as guarantors, but as witnesses to what everyone knew would end up in a lot of false promises. On 16 March 1965 the S.A.N.U. delegates, which included the author, took off for Khartoum, to find on arrival that the status of Mr. Deng was still unsettled. After sitting all night for more than ten hours of heated debate, S.A.N.U. delegates were persuaded by the other Southerners to take Deng as a member. Titles like 'leader of the delegation' were always carefully omitted by the Northern press and members of the Southern Front to avoid embarrassment, because while S.A.N.U. maintained that Mr. Elia Lupe Baraba was their leader, after Mr. Aggrey Jaden's pre-arranged return to Kampala, Mr. Deng persistently called himself the leader.

Negotiations opened with an inaugural address from the Prime Minister, Sir el Khatim el Khalifa, and speeches from heads of the various political parties. While admitting the existence of many differences between the Arabs of the North and the Africans of the South in his inaugural address, Mr. Khalifa tried to assure the observers that the same problem faced Africans everywhere, and that a solution could be a precedent for all Africa. The general theme of the speeches delivered by the heads of the Northern political parties was that the problem should be solved within the framework of a united Sudan, that the problem was an imperialist creation, and that similar ones existed all over Africa. The Southern Front and S.A.N.U.'s stand was that any solution that did not embody recognition of the principle of self-determination would not last and would therefore be unacceptable to the South. A Government-selected delegation of 'nine persons to represent the different shades of opinion in the South' did not deliver a speech because their Government-appointed spokesman withdrew on the grounds that he had no 'shade of opinion' that differed from what S.A.N.U. and the Southern Front had already outlined. In a letter to the Conference Chairman, Mr. Ambrose Wol stated that he was a member of the Southern Front, and did not know who had suggested his name to this other peculiar delegation. The other eight also declared their unqualified support for S.A.N.U. and the Southern Front, and said that it was virtually an insult to think that they could hold opinions other than those which the Southern public held. This not only embarrassed the Government but annoyed the Northern political parties, who then insisted on bringing in other Southerners who might hold different opinions from the first nine.

Before the problem of Southern representation was resolved, Northerners presented two more difficulties. At the beginning, in fact, it looked as though the conference would never start. Northerners insisted that the objectives of the conference were as follows: 'To investigate the Southern question with a view to reaching an agreement which shall satisfy the *regional interests* of the South as well as the *national interests* of the Sudan' (author's italics).[44] A deadlock was only averted by the head of the Ghanaian observer delegation, Mr. Welbeck, then Minister of Information, who appealed for courage and frankness on both sides. The objectives were then amended to read: 'To investigate the Southern question with a view to reaching an agreement which shall satisfy the *special interests* of the South as well as the *general interests* of the North' (author's italics). Southern attempts to add another section—guarantees—to the effect that a copy of the agreement reached should be deposited with the Organisation of African Unity and the Arab

[44] Draft Rules of Procedure, Round Table Conference, Rule 3: Objectives.

League, met with no success. Northerners contended that
their country was a sovereign state and they could not
submit to anybody's patronage in any form.

Instead of wasting time arguing whether S.A.N.U. or the
Southern Front was the true representative of the South,
the Southern delegates presented the following proposals:

S.A.N.U. and the Southern Front propose a plebiscite in the
Southern Sudan to ascertain what the majority of the people of
the Southern Sudan want. It has been the view of S.A.N.U. and
the Southern Front that the people of the Southern Sudan must
decide their future. They have these possible choices:
 (i) Federation;
 (ii) Unity with the North;
 (iii) Separation (to become an independent state).
 Our proposed plebiscite should satisfy the wishes of everybody
—unionists, separatists and federalists.

The Observer Corps was suggested as a body to supervise the
plebiscite, while S.A.N.U. and the Southern Front would
appeal to the Southern Freedom Fighters for calm. It was
also suggested that the Arab army of occupation be withdrawn to barracks in the North.

At this juncture, Northerners began to lose patience. They
confessed frankly that South–North relations were such that
a plebiscite would definitely separate the South from the
North, and that what they really wanted was to be given
time to correct past mistakes. This was not acceptable to the
Southerners, and as the Northern delegates were reluctant
to put any concrete proposals forward, things looked rather
gloomy for a time. Only the combined efforts of the Chairman and the observers induced the Northern political
parties to devise a proposal. Insisting on 'the continued
existence of the Sudan as one sovereign entity', they proposed a system of local government based on geographical
divisions, which would replace a unitary form of government 'because it has been established that the centralised
system does not cater for the political wishes of the people
of the South'. At the same time they maintained that there
was 'no place in the Sudan for a federal system of govern-

ment . . . because . . . the Sudanese, especially in the North, feel that federation is a step towards separation'.[45]

The Southern delegates did not see anything wrong with this proposal if only the principle of self-determination were embodied in it, and the reaction was, therefore, to include it on their list of possible choices:

    (i) Federation;
    (ii) Unity with the North;
    (iii) Separation;
    (iv) Regional Government.

As the Northern delegates were not prepared to pay heed to the idea of a plebiscite, this created a state of deadlock, which was only overcome after an appeal by the then Nigerian Federal Minister of Mines and Power, Al Haj Yusuf M. Sule, who said, 'it is not the problems that face a nation that matter much; what really matters is *how* the leaders of the nation face those problems'.

Taking advantage of this appeal, the Northern delegates challenged the Southerners to suggest precisely what they felt the South would be content to have. In the words of Mr. Sadiq el Mahdi: 'We are sitting here as leaders of the people, and we have got to be confident that they will accept whatever we do for them. A leader is not to be led from behind.'

Accepting the challenge, a system was proposed which would ensure the independence and sovereignty of the Africans in the Southern Sudan, bearing in mind the need for interdependence with the North—'the general interests of the North'.

It appeared at this stage that the Arabs began to feel that they could not do well at the conference table. All appeals from the observers met with no success, and in the end, both delegations accepted—with some modifications—the first part of the Southern scheme of proposals for immediate implementation. These were reform programmes intended to normalize relations with the North. The failure to find a basis for discussions was accepted and it was agreed that a

[45] Draft Rules of Procedure, op. cit.

twelve-man committee be set to work out such a basis, and report to the conference within three months.

Thus, although the conference, which lasted from 16 to 29 of March, broke up without finding a solution to the problem, it passed resolutions which in themselves embodied part of the solution as well as the hope for reaching a final agreement. Subsequent events, however, showed that the Arabs had only tried to test Southern negotiating ability, gain time and Northern public opinion, and use all the excuses there are in the world to solve the problem in their own way. Although the Southern delegates were perfectly aware of this, the conference hall did not present fertile ground for the expression of suspicions, and they had to look as though they accepted each other's promises.

AFTER THE ROUND TABLE CONFERENCE

In order to describe events following the Round Table Conference, something must be said about the various Southern political parties, many of which came into being after the fall of Abboud.

S.A.N.U., which was founded in 1962, held its first convention in Kampala in November 1964. Already the split with William Deng had become serious enough for him not to attend, and at the convention Aggrey Jaden, formerly Assistant Secretary-General, was elected President, and Philip Pedak Vice-President. After the Round Table Conference Deng did not return to Kampala with the other S.A.N.U. delegates. Instead he founded what amounted to a new party within the Sudan which also took the name S.A.N.U. The confusion of having two S.A.N.U.s continued until August 1965, when the group in exile dropped the name and left Deng's party in sole possession.

The Southern Front, as was mentioned earlier, was a grouping of Southern civil servants and students who were for three or four months after the fall of the military régime the sole body representing Southerners in the Sudan, and who nominated three ministers to the Caretaker Government: Clement Mboro (Minister of the Interior), Hilary Paul Logale (Minister of Works), Ezbon Mondiri (Minister of Communications—later replaced by Gordon Muortat following a violent argument with a Northern telephone operator). In addition, Luigi Adwok was installed as their representative on the five-member Supreme Council of State. The Southern Front started their own daily newspaper in Khartoum, the *Vigilant*, which first went to press on 23 March 1965 and, apart from a six-month ban imposed on it by the Government for its reporting of the Juba and Wau incidents in July of that year, has appeared regularly ever since.

Two other small Southern political parties which started up early in 1965 were the old Liberal Party, revived under the leadership of Stanislaus Paysama and Buth Diu, and the Sudan Unity Party, founded by Santino Deng, a man who had been the sole Southern minister during the Army régime and had completely lost the confidence of the Southern people. These two parties have remained too small to be taken seriously. The same goes for the Southern Peace Party, a group which is merely a front organization for certain Northern politicians. What is tragic, of course, is the way in which the North has been able to divide and fragment the Southern political movement. It is common knowledge that parties making claims contrary to Southern aspirations were heavily financed by the Northern parties and by the Government. The Sudan Unity Party even had, apart from financial support, the actual help of the army in eliminating those people in the South who were opposed to Santino Deng's ideas. Others, like William Deng's S.A.N.U., were supplied with equipment by the Government. Most of the unrepresentative parties' leaders were encouraged to go on visits outside the Sudan in order to misinform people about the Southern problem. This is to be compared with the absolute ban on foreign travel imposed upon other less co-operative Southerners.

The Round Table Conference reached no conclusions but it did adopt several resolutions. These included Southern-ization, where possible, of the administration, police, prisons, and so on; freedom of religion and of missionary activity; freedom to open private schools; the appointment of Southerners, whether Arabic-speaking or not, as head-masters to all Southern schools; and the establishment of a university in the South.[46] A twelve-man committee was appointed to carry on the work of the conference with special reference to possible constitutional solutions, and to watch over the implementation of the resolutions, but the committee never functioned satisfactorily and not one of the resolutions was kept. In fact, the very setting up of the committee gave rise to fresh grievances. The conference had agreed that, of the committee's six Southern members, three should be from within the Sudan and three from the group in exile. But the three from outside never received invitations and when one of them, Peter Akol, arrived of his own accord, he was turned away. Eventually Deng's S.A.N.U. filled the three seats reserved for the exiles, and the Southern Front the other three. The twelve-man committee was supposed to report in three months to a second session of the Round Table Conference, but this session was never in fact convened.

Let us now proceed to the highly controversial elections of April 1965. The major Southern parties, with the exception of Deng's party, were opposed to elections being held in the South, devastated after years of army rule. In the Supreme Council, the view prevailed that elections should not be held in the South until the state of emergency there was lifted. However, Luigi Adwok, with some reluctance, but having been given the assurance that the Southern Front would retain its ministerial posts in the new cabinet, gave his casting vote on the Supreme Council in favour of allowing the North to proceed with elections on its own. The South was to follow later. But unfortunately twenty-one candidates had already registered for Southern constituencies, and when Parliament met they demanded to be seated. Their case was eventually upheld in the courts, and in November these twenty-one so-called 'Southern representatives', who were in fact nonentities and included fourteen Northern merchants living in the South, took their seats. Their

---

[46] See *The Voice of the Southern Sudan* (published by S.A.N.U. in exile from 1962 to 1965) (Vol. 3, no. 1, May 1965) for a full statement of the resolutions.

presence has bedevilled all subsequent negotiations for Southern representation in Parliament.

Following the elections, a new Umma–N.U.P. coalition Government was formed on 9 June under the leadership of Muhammad Ahmed Mahgoub. Despite the previous agreement in the Supreme Council, Mahgoub insisted on having other Southern parties besides the Southern Front represented in the cabinet. This caused the Southern Front to withdraw its nominees both from the cabinet and from the Supreme Council, and the South was represented at ministerial level only by Andrew Wieu and Alfred Wol of S.A.N.U. On the Supreme Council it was represented by Philemon Majok, a former delegate at the Juba Conference of 1947 who had joined the Sudan Unity Party. The two S.A.N.U. ministers resigned, however, upon the appointment of Buth Diu, who they said had no backing in the South. Buth Diu continued, despite the provisional constitutional practice of having at least two Southerners, as the sole Southern representative in the cabinet, as Minister of Animal Resources, until 1966.

In June 1965 the Southern Front became a formally registered political party, with Clement Mboro as President, Gordon Muortat as Vice-President, and Hilary Paul Logale as Secretary-General. It continues today to be recognized, despite many hardships, as the party with by far the widest popular support in the South.

Meanwhile, S.A.N.U. in exile was undergoing some rapid transformations. In June 1965 Joseph Oduho, Father Saturnino,[47] George Kwanai, Pancrasio Ocheng, Marko Rume, and some others broke away from the party and formed the Azania Liberation Front (A.L.F.). (The name Azania was that given to an East African civilization of some 4,000 years ago, and is of only dubious relevance to the Sudan.) An attempt to merge S.A.N.U. and A.L.F.

---

[47] Father Saturnino, although never the leader of any political movement in exile, was in fact the most important figure behind the Southern struggle for independence. Despite reports to the contrary, he remained a Roman Catholic priest until his death, which came on 22 January 1967. For an account of his death, see the *Reporter* (Nairobi), 10 March 1967.

resulted in S.A.L.F. (Sudan Africa Liberation Front), but the marriage was premature. Eventually, a reconciliation was effected between the two in December 1965, the party continuing as A.L.F. with Oduho as President and Jaden as Vice-President.

BLOODSHED IN THE SOUTH

The end of the military régime brought a relaxation of the harsh grip in which the South had been held for six years. Political prisoners were released and more of the administration was 'Southernized' than had ever been the case before. Sunday was even restored to the South. But this state of affairs did not last very long. In the middle of the Round Table Conference the Police Superintendant of Bentiu (Upper Nile), a Dinka named Joel Akech Nhial, was murdered by his own Arab police subordinates, and the resultant threat of a general strike throughout the South almost brought an end to the Conference. In May, Luigi Adwok threatened to resign from the Supreme Council unless an explanation of the killing of several people and the burning of his own village in Upper Nile Province was forthcoming. And shortly after the installation of Mahgoub's government, in July, came the bloodiest attacks on Southerners yet witnessed.

The night of 8 July will long be remembered with bitterness by the town of Juba. Although there is evidence that the army had received instructions some days before to liquidate all educated Southerners in the town, the actual incident which started the mass killing was an argument over a transistor radio between an army sergeant in civvies and a Southerner who was a dresser at the local hospital. The sergeant received injuries, and when news of this reached the Arab soldiers, who were returning from the cinema at 10 p.m., they took their weapons from the armoury and started systematically to burn and to kill. By morning all the 3,000 or so grass-thatched houses of the five Southern sectors of the town had been burned, and their inhabitants were either dead, in hiding, or in refuge in Juba cathedral. The soldiers even went to the operating theatre of the local hospital and shot the patient on the table, though the doctor escaped by jumping out the window. No one knows for certain how many died. The official police figure was 1,019,[48] but the real number was probably more than 1,400. Northern politicians habitually put the total at less than a hundred. The suspicion that there was a deliberate Government plot to kill all actual and potential leaders in the South is confirmed by the fact that after the massacre, the acting Governor of Equatoria, Sayed Ahmed Hassan, went to the hospital and the cemeteries with the Commandant of Police. They had a list of names, and at each place inquired whether the dead included, amongst others, various officials and members of the Southern Front.

The massacre at Juba was closely followed by a smaller though equally shocking killing at Wau. There the army chose as a setting the reception following a double wedding ceremony. Mr. Ottavio Deng and his cousin Cypriano Cier were married on 11 July in Wau Cathedral to two sisters, daughters of Chief Benjamin Lang. At the reception afterwards a soldier entered and quietly asked four Northerners present to leave. Then, according to the eye-witness report of James Yol, the horrified guests discovered that the house was surrounded by soldiers, who immediately opened fire. In all seventy-six people died, including one of the bridegrooms.

These two mass killings at Juba and Wau were enough to convince Southerners of the true intentions of the Sudan Government, and the resulting cycle of panic, retaliation, and counter-retaliation quickly reduced the three Southern provinces to a state of anarchy. Refugees fled across the frontiers into Ethiopia, Kenya, Uganda, the Congo, and the Central African Republic in such quantities that the total number of Southern Sudanese exiles was estimated to be over 100,000 in 1965. As in Abboud's era, the Anya-Nya harassed the army constantly, but this time with modern automatic weapons instead of spears and bows and arrows. These weapons were a windfall resulting from the rebellion

[48] Reported in a letter to *The Times* from Peter Kilner in Khartoum, 27 November 1965.

in the Congo where the sequence of events seems to have been as follows.

In July 1964, the Congolese 'simbas' under Christopher Gbenye revolted against the Government of Moise Tshombe. Certain African States, such as Algeria and the United Arab Republic, decided to aid the rebels, and with the help of Khartoum large quantities of arms were shipped to them through the Southern Sudan. As it turned out, however, the simbas were defeated, and from May to November 1965 many of them fled back across the frontier into the Sudan, abandoning their guns or selling them to the Anya-Nya for food. Weapons are indeed a double-edged sword!

Thus armed, the freedom fighters were able to seize control of the countryside, and restrict Northern military influence to the towns. Bridges were blown up, and in many cases the only communication between army outposts was by air. Unfortunately though, only too often the real sufferers were neither the army nor the Anya-Nya but the civilians. A graphic illustration of this came in October 1965, when the Anya-Nya attacked and destroyed the steamer *Abu Anga* at Tewfikia. In retaliation the army massacred eighty-nine innocent villagers (all males) from Warajwok, three miles south of Malakal. This pattern of attack and retaliation has become familiar through constant repetition over the last two years. Occasionally there is a variation, as when the army burns a village first. The Anya-Nya have then been known to burn whatever houses are still standing, acting on the theory that their owners must be collaborating with the Arabs. In either cases, it is the ordinary people who suffer.

As the months of 1965 passed, bitter fighting continued between the two sides. Bombers were occasionally used by the North, though it was reported that their British pilots had little heart for the work. In the first week of August the Anya-Nya surrounded seventy soldiers in the Tembura district of Equatoria Province, and parachute troops had to be flown from Khartoum to rescue them. An offer by President Nkrumah of Ghana to mediate between North and South was refused by Khartoum on the grounds that the problem was entirely internal. The Anya-Nya set up their own crude system of government in the South to replace the administration that (except in the towns) had vanished, and collected their own taxes. Both sides prepared themselves for a long struggle.

The conflict was a bitter but silent one, for the most part entirely concealed from the outside world. Only occasionally would the curtain be lifted, as when a journalist managed to penetrate illegally into the Southern Sudan. The first such journalist was François Chauvel of *Le Figaro*, who spent six weeks living and travelling with the Anya-Nya. His account appeared in *Le Figaro*. Two other French reporters, Claude Deffarge and Gordian Troeller, followed in the steps of Chauvel and wrote their story in *Le Nouvel Observateur* of 8 March 1967. Thirdly, an English reporter, Anthony Carthew, visited the headquarters of the Anya-Nya in eastern Equatoria, at the same time that Chauvel was in the area, and published his report in the *Daily Mail* of 31 January, 1 and 2 February 1966. His account began: 'Here an entire people is dying. Here a race war of immense ferocity is being fought.' This is no exaggeration of what is happening in the Southern Sudan.

SADIQ'S TERM OF OFFICE

In June 1966 there occurred an event which many people hoped would lead to a lessening of tension and to a more constructive approach on the part of the Sudan Government. This was the replacement of Premier Mahgoub by Sayed Sadiq el Mahdi, who at 30 became the youngest Prime Minister in the world. Many people regarded Sadiq as an enlightened leader who would do his best to solve the grave problems that beset his country. In fact he was incapable of doing this, as subsequent events showed.

Nevertheless, one of Sadiq's first actions with regard to the South was to remove Buth Diu from the cabinet and replace him by two civil servants, Arop Yor Ayik and Jervase Yak. Furthermore, the Sudan told its North African partners in the U.N. Economic Commission for Africa, which included the U.A.R., Libya, Tunisia, Algeria, and Morocco, that it wanted to transfer to the East African group. This was a significant move in view of the Government's insistence that the Sudan was an Arab country, and as such was an integral part of the Arab League. But in all important respects Sadiq's actions indicated that he had not abandoned the hope that the Southern problem could be solved by coercion rather than negotiation.[49] This is best shown by his attempts to impose a constitution unwelcome to the South.

Throughout 1966 Sadiq pressed hard for elections to be held in the South. The purpose of these elections was clearly to enable Parliament to act in the capacity of a constituent assembly and approve a constitution for the country. (The Sudan is the only African country which still lacks a constitution.) The twelve-man committee which was the legacy of the Round Table Conference worked for over a year on constitutional problems, and finally presented its report in September 1966. At that time the Chairman, Sayed Yousif Mohamed Ali, stated that there was agreement that the present *status quo*—centralized unitary government—could no longer serve the country's national interest.[50] Though the report was never published,[51] it seems there was disagreement amongst the delegates over the type and degree of decentralization desirable. The Southern delegates wanted the South to be treated as a unit or single region in whatever system was eventually adopted, while the Northerners favoured a certain degree of local autonomy based on the present system of division into provinces.

Although the next logical step after the presenting of the report would have been the reconvening of the Round Table Conference to consider it, Sadiq instead decided to call into existence a new Constitutional Draft Committee. On this committee Southern representation was to be considerably reduced: thus Umma, N.U.P., P.D.P., and independent

---

[49] Though compare the remark of the military commander in the South, Major-General Ahmed el-Sharif, who early in 1966 told the journalist Keith Kyle that 'there has got to be a political solution'. (*Sunday Nation* (Nairobi), 27 March 1966.)

[50] *Vigilant* (Khartoum), 27 September 1966.

[51] Mimeographed copies of the report were, however, distributed to the political parties.

Northerners would each have seven members. The Islamic Charter Front five, and the Nuba independents two. Compared to this, the South would have only seven in all: two from the Southern Front, two from S.A.N.U., and one each from the Sudan Unity Party, the Liberal Party, and the Southern Peace Party. Needless to say the Southern Front and S.A.N.U. decided not to send delegates under these conditions; the P.D.P. declined likewise; and the remaining parties were left to argue the vexed question of whether the Sudan should have an Islamic constitution. A hint of what was in store for the country if such a constitution were adopted was provided by Dr. Turabi, the Secretary General of the Islamic Charter Front. This gentleman in an evening of discussion with the Southern Front and S.A.N.U. asked why, if the Western European powers had hitherto dominated Africa, had the Muslim countries not the right to try and get their ideas to replace Western ideas and religion? When Mr. Alier of the Southern Front pointed out that in history during the Islamic ascendency the highest office held by a non-Muslim was that held by a Greek accountant, Dr. Turabi replied that the Muslims in the Sudan were in a majority anyway and that in such a situation a Southerner should not pretend to aspire to hold the highest office of state.[52]

As was stated above, the main reasons for holding elections in the remaining Southern constituencies was to push through parliamentary approval for a constitution. The Southern Front, on the other hand, took the position that elections should be held only *after* agreement had been reached on a new constitution, and that in any case elections were impossible while a state of emergency existed in the South. Nevertheless, preparations for elections were made, and despite a report from the P.D.P. in Khartoum that the polling lists, which were made up from chiefs' old tax registers, including the dead, the absent, and the refugee, and that the activities of the Anya-Nya made it almost impossible for some candidates to visit their constituencies, the elections were held on 8 March 1967. The Southern

[52] *Vigilant*, 16 October 1966.

F

Front maintained its boycott, while S.A.N.U. participated. The results in thirty-six constituencies were as follows (the polling in three constituencies was cancelled because they were under Anya-Nya control, and, as mentioned above, the remaining twenty-one Southern members were seated 'unopposed' in 1965).

Umma	15	
S.A.N.U.	10	(including Deng)
N.U.P.	5	
Independents	3	(including Adwok)
Unity Party	2	
Liberal Party	1	(Buth Diu)

RECENT DEVELOPMENTS

By its original writ, the Parliament which was elected in April, and which started its sessions in June 1965, was due to come to an end in June 1967. Sadiq was in favour of extending its life for another two years, but on 15 May 1967 he was defeated in a vote of confidence, and was replaced by Mahgoub as Premier. For some time there appeared to be what many people liked to describe as a 'change of heart' on Mahgoub's part. Some of the spirit of co-operation which prevailed in 1964–5 between Sir el Khatim's Caretaker Government and the Southern Front, and which had been destroyed by Mahgoub himself, seemed to have been restored. It is worth examining the motives underlying this spirit of co-operation between the Southern Front and a man who, only six months earlier, had believed that he could solve the Southern question by force.

As was admitted by a prominent member of the Southern Front, any move taken by a Northern leader must be viewed with great suspicion. There is an open struggle for power within the Umma Party which has resulted in a big rift between the Imam el Hadi (Sadiq el Mahdi's uncle) and Sadiq. The Imam, as traditional head of the Ansar religious sect, feels that he is the rightful presidential candidate, should the Sudan adopt a presidential constitution. Young Sadiq el Mahdi, on the other hand, is too ambitious to abandon hopes for a post to which he regards himself as the heir. This struggle between uncle and nephew gave the N.U.P. and the P.D.P. every opportunity to fish successfully for support among the intellectuals in the Southern Sudan.

The Imam's Umma wing soon realized that Sadiq had made a mistake in thinking that S.A.N.U. had a large intellectual following in the South. The fact was that S.A.N.U.'s following consisted largely of young adventurers who posed as intellectuals, while most of the highly respected Southern politicians and intellectuals were in the Southern Front. The Imam's wing of Umma, the P.D.P., and the N.U.P. all therefore decided to court the Southerners—each hoping in their own way to gain support from the latter. Meanwhile, preparations went on vigorously for elections in early 1968.

The Southern Front's motives for co-operation also need mentioning. As long as some freedom of speech prevailed in the North, where they were clustered, they could speak their minds freely for the South. But since that freedom was totally lacking in the South, it grew more difficult for them to contact their own followers. There was (and still is at the time of writing) always the danger of a stray bullet from a Northerner in the South, which is explained by the 'security forces' as being from 'outlaws'. They therefore had had little contact with their followers since the Round Table Conference. However, they maintained a great deal of the spirit and determination of the Conference. Their main problem was how to play safe politics with the Arabs without condemning themselves to exile or taking big risks. A few (like Gordon Muortat, who was Minister of Communications in the Caretaker Government) chose exile. His predecessor, Ezbon Mondiri, had already left the country in disgust.

Southern political parties which co-operated with the Arab North did not have anything to fear. They went to the South and to foreign countries to preach their belief at will. They were in fact guarded and given full protection by the army against their own people, the 'outlaws'. Once back in Khartoum, they said they had been in contact with 'the people', and they claimed to know better than the Southern Front what the people in the South wanted. Such claims attracted many weak-willed and highly credulous people. Southern public opinion in the North was diluted, and there was a great danger of everybody drifting away from the Southern Front which still symbolized Southern aspirations.

Faced with the problem of being isolated in Khartoum from their own public, and being uncertain of what the masses of Southerners in exile and the rural areas would be content with, the Southern Front decided to contest the elections. Contacts with the group in exile (through whom it was possible to pass a message into the jungles where the masses of the people lived) appeared to have resulted in a rift between the two. The two groups had hitherto agreed to differ in technique, but showed clearly that they had the same aim. However, the Southern Front had moved from its original position of 'no elections in the South until the state of emergency has been lifted and the constitutional question resolved', to one where they accepted elections, first, because the mass of Southerners were getting worn out, and might therefore be led astray by S.A.N.U. and the like; secondly, because once in Parliament, they hoped to be able to prevent the adoption of a constitution which ignored the rights of the Southern people; and thirdly, because no single political party in the Sudan is able to form a Government, and they might therefore negotiate themselves into a coalition with a party which would appreciate the Southern case.

One of the reasons which helped to harden the position of the group in exile was that the Southern Front leaders began to dance to the same propaganda tune which they had hitherto condemned—'Conditions in the South are back to normal', they proclaimed. Although this helped them to retain the support of their remaining Khartoum followers, as well as work them into a mood for the elections, it now seems clear that they have lost face in the South. Conditions might not have been as bad as when they condemned them, but they were (and still are) certainly far from being 'back to normal'.

In the North, after some negotiations, the National

Unionist Party (N.U.P.) and the People's Democratic Party (P.D.P.) merged towards the end of 1967 to form what is now called the Unionist Democratic Party (U.D.P.). The leader of the N.U.P., Sayed Ismail el Azhari, appeared to have outlived his views of a secular state, and was advocating an Islamic constitution. The question of closer links with Egypt had already taken him at the head of his party delegation to Cairo after the Round Table Conference. There were therefore hardly any differences between these two parties. They had been one before 1956. When they reunited, Sayed Azhari became President, and Ali Abdul Rahman of the P.D.P. Vice-President. Apart from the fact that the P.D.P. and the Umma are traditional rivals (both parties are associated with rival religious sects) the formation of the U.D.P. has managed to weaken the Umma Party very considerably.

The U.D.P., therefore, is really a coalition between two parties with only Azhari's personality and the fear of the Umma Party acting as cohesive forces. It has two policies: Azhari's and Sayed Ali Mirghani's names. (Sayed Ali Mirghani, the former patron of the P.D.P., died in February 1968.) This lack of clear motives in the merger showed itself in the 1968 elections. It was not uncommon for two U.D.P. candidates to rival each other in a constituency. Such internal rivalries were best exploited by the Sudan Communist Party, who returned a candidate from Atbara constituency at the expense of the U.D.P., and whose leader, Abdel Khalig, defeated a former U.D.P. Minister, Mohammed Zein Abdeen, at Omdurman.

In the South the state of emergency which was declared by Azhari's N.U.P. Government in 1955 is still in force. It was only slightly relaxed in 1958 for the elections. But it has always been there, and people have only managed to defy it to varying degrees with varying consequences.

As I have tried to explain in this book, North–South relations are marred by mutual suspicion and Southern lack of confidence in the Northern administration. A visit to the South at the time of writing will at once reveal that it is in a state of administrative and governmental disruption. Arab administration is only effective in towns. The rural areas have been reduced to human hunting grounds where the defenceless people who take refuge in the surrounding forests are shot on sight by the Northern soldiers who occasionally go on patrols. Parts of the countryside have reverted back to tribal organization, while others, under the complete control of the Freedom Fighters, have set up an administrative system geared to meet the immediate needs of the people. Of course the degree of sophistication of this administration varies from one area to another, according to the availability of personnel and equipment. With the continual air and ground raids on villages by Arab troops of occupation, people tend to move away from the roads. Consequently, the once prosperous rural areas which were linked to the towns by motor roads are rapidly turning into impassable jungles. Rural dispensaries are abandoned. People who venture into towns for medical treatment are at once suspected as 'outlaws'; hence an increasing number turn to the Freedom Fighters who are only able to give simple first-aid treatment. There is no doubt that the entire rural population places its confidence in the Freedom Fighters, hence the Freedom Movement as a whole. It is their hope for the future as a Black African state. At least it has shown that an externally imposed state of anarchy can be removed by a Southern administration.

The formation of a provisional government in the Southern Sudan had therefore had great psychological effects on the people. They feel more secure than they did under a political movement in exile, which had questionable authority over the Freedom Fighters, and which was set up without consultation with them. This government was inaugurated at Angudri in the Southern Sudan on 18 August 1967, and later transferred to Bungu. This was clearly an answer to the question which was lurking in the minds of the Reconciliation Committee between A.L.F. and S.A.L.F. at Kampala— how to keep the movement united. A political party cannot ban or outlaw the possibility of the formation of other political parties. But a government can. People who disagreed with S.A.N.U.—in most cases because they had not been offered posts or the titles they thought most suited to them—simply went ahead and formed A.L.F. But these splinter activities are not possible now, or have at least been greatly minimized, because people recognize the fact that a government is different from a party. It is not easy to set up a rival government without first enlisting the support of the Freedom Fighters and that of the people. (Ezbon Mondiri has since tried to establish a rival government based in East Africa, but has failed.)

Under the Provisional Government, the country is divided into nine regions under Regional Commissioners or Chairmen. Each region is in turn divided into District Councils under District Commissioners or Chairmen. These are responsible to the Regional Commissioners who are in turn responsible to the dual Government and military headquarters (where the President sits for the day-to-day civil administration of the country). The districts are in turn organized into Village Councils. Wherever possible, every village is supplied with home guards to protect the civil population from being molested by Arab troops. This gives the people confidence to settle and carry out their cultivation of the land. The obvious effect of this organization has been to unify the Freedom Movement at home and to enable people to turn a deaf ear to dissenting politicians in exile. At best, they are asked to go 'home' and 'work for the people' if they wish to be leaders.

The greatest problem facing the Provisional Government is lack of publicity. Perhaps many readers will find its existence completely fresh news. Many people still do not even know that a problem exists in the Sudan. I have met some who think we are to blame for lack of publicity. I accept some of this blame, but not all of it. When you meet a newsman, his Government is either very friendly with the Sudan Government, or he has a vain hope at the back of his mind of being allowed into the Southern Sudan by the Sudan Government to verify your story and so will not jeopardize his chances. He will therefore either publish only the most obvious part of the facts, or make very mild and a very dubious story out of a very serious situation. In most cases, the Southern story is simply shelved as unreasonable, and newsmen quote back what the Sudan Government says. Indeed, three things are necessary to be heard: first of all, a strong striking force, and secondly, a wireless transmitter like Biafra. The third possibility is to fight an ideological war like the Vietnamese and the Viet Cong. The Southern movement has hitherto largely depended for its publicity on the group in exile. Some of these people misconducted themselves, resulting in censorship by the host governments of anti-Sudan Government utterances. Only occasionally does the story of the Southern Sudan claim a few lines in the press, yet unless the Provisional Government tackles this problem urgently, the war will be prolonged, with all the possibilities of genocide facing the population.

Apart from the declared results, little is known to the outside world about the 1968 Elections. But it is anyone's guess as to what elections can be under a state of emergency and martial law in an area where the Government forces are clearly aware that they are fighting against the political aspirations of the people.

Very few people turned up at the polling stations. Many of these were captured from exile and kept in special voters' camps ('Peace Camps') where they were told what to do. These voters sometimes included non-Southern Sudanese from neighbouring countries who were captured by the troops by mistake. In any case, the highest known number of voters for any candidate in any constituency was 4,910 in Tonj Central Constituency where William Deng was elected. Some of these were Northern soldiers, policemen, and prison wardens who constituted the real voting population in these elections. The winning candidate in one of the Torit constituencies amassed a total of thirty votes, and in Kajo-Kaji the winner received ninety-five.

Where a Southern candidate was particularly unpopular (as was the case in Southern Yei where Mr. Lubari Ramba Lokolo stood), up to twelve puppet candidates were encouraged to contest the elections. This, of course, confused the voters by dividing the few votes in such a way that the military contingent in that area formed the largest number of electorates favouring a particular candidate.

This begs the question as to whether the elections were rigged or not. The reader will discover an answer for himself out of the following facts:

(i) Some of the captured electors were given £S3 as inducement money to vote for the Government-supported candidate. Somehow, seventeen people at Lasu, four at Kaya, and one at Iwatoka polling stations did not vote for the official candidates. They were arrested and their inducement money reclaimed.

(ii) Mr. Hilary Paul Logale (formerly Minister of Labour and Social Services) lost one of his ballot boxes—reports say it was burnt by some angry soldiers who thought that the box would have made the difference.

(iii) The elections were held from 18 to 25 April 1968 and the results were not ready until 7 p.m. on 6 May 1968. It is a case for either admitting that conditions are not back to normal for easy communications or that the results were being reconsidered and monitored in Khartoum.

(iv) The army deliberately held up Southern candidates for three constituencies in the Kapoeta area (apparently because of 'transport difficulties') on the nomination day. This move was calculated to return the Government-appointed candidates unopposed, since there were no other nominees.

Apart from these incidents, the puritan Christian sect called Balokole was openly employed in Yei district as a propaganda instrument for the Arab-favoured candidates. Their message to the electorates was naïve: 'You know the government is strong, and if you vote for the Southern candidate, you will all be shot. We want peace. Don't let people who live with Satan in the bush deceive you. They will never win, for they have nothing compared with what the government has. Where is their money?' These people were well protected, and given adequate facilities not only to live comfortably, but also to move about easily. Lubari Luö, Chief Luö's son, was used by the army to terrorize

Southerners in the Government's own 'Peace Camps', and said similar things to those said by the Balokole.

The results for the whole country were as follows:

Unionist Democratic Party	101
Umma–Sadiq	38
Umma–Imam	30
S.A.N.U.	15
Southern Front	10
Islamic Charter Front	3
Sudan Communist Party	2
Independents	10
Local parties	6
Total	215

Three constituencies in the South were too unsettled for elections. In addition to the twenty-five M.P.s belonging to the combined force of S.A.N.U. and the Southern Front, four Southern independents were elected, but this still leaves the majority of the sixty Southern constituencies returning M.P.s who are members of Northern parties. (Sixteen of Sadiq's total of thirty-eight come in fact from the South.) When one appreciates this fact, one realizes with how small a voice the South actually speaks in the new Parliament. It is worth noting, however, that both Santino Deng and Buth Diu were defeated.

Immediately after the elections, on the 5 May 1968, a tragic event occurred, one which symbolizes a great deal concerning North–South relations in the Sudan today. William Deng, President of S.A.N.U., was murdered along with six of his supporters in an ambush on the Rumbek-Wau road by members of the Hajjana (Camel Corps) unit. About a week later, the world was misinformed through Radio Omdurman that Mr. Deng had been killed by the 'outlaws'. This remains the official version of his death outside the Sudan. In the Sudan it is common knowledge that he was killed by Government forces, and although investigations were ordered to determine the motives behind this savage act, only optimists are expecting a report. As evidence of governmental collusion, one notes that on 7 May nearly all the houses of S.A.N.U. candidates in Rumbek were cordoned off by the Arab troops and fired at. In fact the Secretary-General of S.A.N.U., Samuel Aru, was presumed killed for a long time afterwards.

The Government formed under Premier Mahgoub in late May 1968 was a coalition between the U.D.P., Umma–Imam, and the Southern Front. Philemon Majok was succeeded on the Supreme Council by Jervase Yak, and the two Southern ministers were Clement Mboro (Mines and Industry) and Hilary Paul Logale (Labour and Social Services). In the opposition, Umma–Sadiq and S.A.N.U. had a certain understanding to work together. But life in the South continues much as before. The goal aimed at by successive Arab Governments is annexation and loose assimilation under the morally accepted name of unity. On the other hand, the average Southern Sudanese nationalist seeks to obtain recognition of the principle of self-determination for the Southern Sudan. This must not be taken only to mean independence for the South, because the South could easily determine its future identity with the North.

This is where we have a tug-of-war with the Arabs in the Northern Sudan. Many of them are beginning to admit that there is an acute problem which needs a political solution. But they always have a fixed solution. For example, Mohammed Omer Beshir, who seems to have written most liberally on the matter, thinks that the Southern problem must be solved within the context of a united Sudan— mainly for economic and historical reasons.[53] Many Southerners, on the other hand, see the danger of fighting an un-publicized war as well as that of being isolated by world public opinion. These facts have brought the Southern Front and some Northerners to a common ground where, even if they disagree, each side will rest content that world public opinion will at least believe that it has gone out of its way for co-operation. That is probably why the Southern Front is in the Government today, if we are to believe

[53] Mohammed Omer Beshir, *The Southern Sudan: Background to Conflict* (London, Hurst, 1968).

Mohammed Omer Beshir's statement that they are 'seccessionists'.

The Southern Front leaders, however, try to explain their motives as being 'to try to inform the government and the public at large of the situation in the South and to direct its decisions, as far as possible, so that they do not adversely affect the South'. They admit that this is a virtually impossible task, but they have to do it because world public opinion is more inclined to believe explanations for failure of co-operation than to accept predictions based on experience. There is also the fear that a Sudan Government without genuine Southern politicians will give a chance to Northern politicians to build up puppet leaders for the South—a fact which has been in process for so long that there are already quite a number of such leaders.

The Northern leaders, on the other hand, see and use the present situation of the Southern Front as a weapon for ridiculing the Southern case. The Southern Sudan Provisional Government is at war with the Arab Government in Khartoum. Seated in the Khartoum Government are Southern Sudanese leaders voting money for the war! Obviously, this strengthens Arab arguments that Southerners are fighting against a legally constituted government. I am not condemning anybody. This is simply how I see it. The Southern Front needs to re-state its policy to suit its activities.

III | An Epitome from Experience

There is an inborn feeling of dislike and uneasiness in every Southerner about the *mundukuru* or *jallaba*—Southern names for the Northern Sudanese Arabs. The British, unconsciously or otherwise, kept this feeling from bursting into flames by a policy of separate or decentralized administration for the Southern Sudan since the conquest of the Sudan in 1898. In 1902—only three years after the promulgation of the Condominium rule—this took the more definite form of a policy for the South (since 1930 commonly referred to as Southern Policy). But the mere fact that the British permitted Arab merchants to trade in the South, gave them liberty to build mosques, and recruited some to work in the offices, was enough to keep the fire smouldering.

In the early days of my life, in my home town of Juba, I had the strange feeling that the mission of the white man in Africa was to see that the Arabs and the Africans did not quarrel. The Arab and African communities were always separated. In cases where an Arab married a Southern girl—a rare, unrecipocated phenomenon—it was looked upon with scorn by African neighbours, and was considered as only a temporary or pleasure marriage, since the Arab invariably left the woman and the children in the South when going to the North.

No doubt, the history of the slave trade which was passed orally from one generation to another, played a great part in determining such relations. But the main thing is that the Arabs behaved as constant reminders of the past. They too must have had their share of oral traditions. Perhaps in the eyes of my exact Arab counterpart, the British were not acting as guarantors to stop a clash, but were actually depriving them of a possession—the Africans.

Together with my playmates, I used to go to the mosque on Muslim feast days to enjoy the festivities. Although this was purely out of childish curiosity, we were never really too childish or too curious to mix with Arab boys even inside the mosque. On the contrary, there were occasions when clashes took place between the African and the Arab children, resulting in throwing stones and wounding one another. The traditional Arab way of degrading a person is to take a slipper or a shoe off his foot and beat the person with it. This is supposed to indicate that the person so beaten is completely 'under one's feet'. Most of the incidents arose from such insults. Such an attack on one African child was considered an attack on all, and nobody bothered to find out the reasons for the fight. It is very difficult to express such attitudes in rational terms, but reason and sentiment do not always agree.

After the Juba Conference of 1947, in which the British decided to reverse the policy of separate administration for the South, some anxious Northern officials in Juba started evening classes for the Arabic language. At the same time, the language was introduced in the intermediate schools. I was then in the fourth year at Juba Church Missionary Society (C.M.S.) Elementary Venacular School, hoping to go to the intermediate school the following year. By force of circumstances, I joined the evening classes in the official's club. One day one of my teachers, a certain Ligani, decided either to give or to reward me with one of his children's shirts and a pair of shorts. At first, I welcomed the present because I honestly needed some clothes. On my way home, however, I began to weigh the fact that these clothes were not only given by a *mudukuru*, but had been used by one too! What would I tell my friends? With a deep feeling of guilt and humiliation, I returned to my teacher, and asked him to take the clothes back until I had permission from my father to accept them. When he asked why, I told him that my father was very strict and he might suspect I had stolen the clothes. My teacher offered to go and explain the gift to my father, but I told him that it was no use because my father was on a trip.

One of the biggest mistakes the Arabs in the Sudan make is to suspect everybody of inciting the Africans. I personally feel that we all evolved sets of ideas about the *jallabas*, whether we had grandmothers to relate the stories of the Arab raids or not. However, my grandmother is still alive. My father, who in 1916, only seventeen years after the Condominium Government was set up, joined the Egyptian Army after several years' service as the tribal chief's personal guard, died in 1966. When I was born, he was already on a pension, and was completely grey haired. The reader can judge for himself whether my best teacher on the past would be a 21-year-old missionary, fresh from the United Kingdom, on a twentieth-century adventure to Africa, or my grandmother and father. No doubt the missionaries were a most effective force in promoting the policies of the Colonia Office and, while a policy of separate administration existed, they might have worked to ensure that Northerners and Southerners did not have any feelings of fraternity. This is an affair for those who were old enough before 1947 to argue about. For my generation, we had our own secret (and sometimes suppressed) anti-missionary feelings when they advocated 'love for all mankind' in order to impose the 1947 agreement on us. They went as far as to tell us that we were too poor to do without the Northerners. Northerners will not willingly admit this.

In 1948 I was one of the lucky forty or so, out of about 2,000, to find a place in the intermedate school. In 1951, when Mr. Sir El Khatim El Khalifa—Prime Minister of the Care-Taker Government from October 1964 to June 1965—was visiting schools on his take-over inspection from Mr. Johnson Smith as the Assistant Director of Education in the Southern Provinces, a colleague of mine asked whether the Arabs were aware that they were imposing a state of independence on the Sudan while the South was underdeveloped and least ready for it. Mr. Khalifa gave an answer which I think was intelligently evasive. He said: 'It is natural every human being and country should try to be independent.' But the two Britons—the outgoing Assistant Director of Education, Mr. Johnson Smith, and the headmaster, Mr. Ian H. Watts—lost their temper. The headmaster angrily told the class that the South was too small—which is untrue—and too poor—which we accept—to remain aloof while the North went ahead with independence. We all got emotionally involved in this irrelevant talk, and I pointed out to the headmaster that we felt more akin to Uganda and Kenya than we did to the North, and if it pleased the British Government, we would prefer to be annexed to Uganda or Kenya. My friend (who must remain anonymous) got excited and shouted, 'Yes, and form part of East Africa.' The headmaster was obviously embarrassed, and shouted to my friend to keep quiet or get out. Mr. Johnson Smith, looking very wise but obviously disturbed, shouted in an angry tone, 'If you join Uganda or Kenya, now that Uganda and Kenya are very rich and advanced, what are you going to offer?' There was an uneasy silence in the class. He stared at me, looked round and repeated, 'What are you going to offer?' I ventured an answer: 'What have we offered to be united with the Northerners, Sir?' I was badly rebuked by the headmaster, and warned never again to be so rude to important Government officials or I would be dismissed from the school. I was forced to admit that I was wrong because it was politics, and I was only a schoolboy. Although this admission of guilt was very serious and sincere on my part, I still felt independence for the Sudan at that stage coming like a falling roof on a closed room. We were the victims in the room, and had to decide what to do.

If there was anything political I learnt in Rumbek Secondary School, it was defiance of anybody who tried to convince me there was nothing Southerners should be afraid of, because whatever they wanted would be easily resolved after independence. In 1952, while in my first year, I drafted a few points in my pocket note-book, with a view to elaborating on them in a letter to Southern Members of Parliament, denouncing those who had joined Northern political parties and calling upon the rest for firm action.

I do not know how the book got into the hands of Mr. Crichton, the headmaster. All I now remember is that he called me into his office, smiled, and handed it back to me, asking whether he was right to assume that it was mine. Although I answered in the affirmative, I never had the courage to write the letter, since it was already discovered.

Our troubles appeared to increase with Sudanization—which meant replacing the British by the Arabs from the North. The new headmaster, Mr. Abdel Rahman, who was certainly one of Ismail El Azhari's special selections for the South, found himself entangled in preaching anti-British doctrines to the students, even when they made it very clear to him that it was then a question of choosing between two evils. The British had mostly left, and the rest were leaving. But the big question in the minds of Southerners at the time was: 'Would their successors not revert to Mahdism?'

In 1955, the Southern revolt broke out,[1] and schools in the South were closed for a year—for no reason other than malice. Although the Government's finances were already running precariously low after paying all the compensations to the outgoing British officials, they chose to transport school desks, chairs, blackboards, tables, and so on, with all the students of Rumbek and Juba Commercial Secondary Schools and Maridi Teachers' Training College to occupy the evacuated British barracks in Khartoum. Our immediate reaction was to protest to the Government in the strongest possible terms, indicating that the only interpretation we could find was that this was a deportation order. With many armed Southern soldiers still at large, we also suspected that the Government's intention was to keep us as hostages; for we were variously described by Khartoum newspapers as 'sons of mutineers', 'murderers', and 'savages'. At this time we had another headmaster, a mean personality who was virtually a social outcast in the North, and best known to Northern students as 'Bismark'. He could not do any worse than the students would have expected an Arab Northerner to behave towards Southerners. All his speeches to the

[1] For an account of the revolt, see Chapter 2, p. 38.

G

school can best be summarized as reminding Southerners that Northerners were only too kind to treat them as citizens instead of taking them straight from the British as subjects. I once quoted one of his speeches verbatim in a letter to the Minister of Education during a students' strike in 1956. At first he was determined to dismiss me from the school (having been told by his informers that I wrote the letter), but on learning that I had been enrolled as a private candidate for the Oxford School Certificate, and was really only passing time in the school, he thought the greatest harm he could do was to tell me that I had to wait and sit for the Sudan School Certificate, whether I liked it or not, because the University of Khartoum might not recognize an Oxford Certificate. There was no point in making such a declaration because I had decided to sit for both examinations anyway.

At this time, a group of secret editors sprang up in the school with three wall-papers. One was called the *Daily Spark*, another, the *Evening Star*, and the third, the *Morning Prayer*. We all made our various contributions without knowing who the editors were. Neither the headmaster's agents nor the staff could trace anybody. These papers set out to explain what an average Southerner felt, and what he thought should be the ultimate solution. They even predicted further violence and spared no terms in describing the Northerners as 'imperialists' and 'power thirsty'. No doubt such concerted actions won the school its return to the South within two years of exile. Maridi Teachers' College, which was relatively docile, is still in exile.

If Southerners who had stood firm for a federal system of government for the Sudan were described by Northern politicians as a 'half-educated' few, whose views were not shared by the Southern masses and élite, then I suppose those of us who went to the Khartoum University and elsewhere were 'quarter-educated' or less. The gap grew wider the closer we came to the Arabs, and the reader can imagine what pains one felt in sharing the same premises, lecture rooms, and students' club with those for whom one had so much resentment. The worst of it came when one had to suppress these feelings, cover them with an academic cloak, and pretend to be reasonable, or even friendly. Although physical clashes were always avoided, many wall-papers did what they could to represent the views of students on both sides. We were still savages and even 'half-educated', according to our own Arab colleagues. We, in turn, tried to portray them as barbarous imperialists, people who were thirsty for power, desirous to dominate and rule, but unable to manage even their own fundamental affairs.

Our own organ for the Student's Welfare Front—the name for the Southern students' group in Khartoum University—was given the emotional name of *Negro*. Although the *Negro* was as extreme as we could have wished it to be, and although as the then Chief Editor I thought we had maintained a 'true Southern spirit' in the paper, many of my colleagues were not quite happy about the discussions that took place on every article prior to publication. We could not be perfect, because some of us were infatuated with certain ideas which we had picked up from some leaflets in Khartoum. Instead of concentrating on our cause, we were being asked to think about the 'workers' in general. Our primary question in the South is 'Where are the workers?' There is not even work. The Northerners prefer to concentrate all schemes in the North so as to solve their own unemployment problems while leaving the South chronically unemployed. Such feelings of lack of oneness, caused by the inevitable factor that in any organization disagreements are bound to occur, sparked off another paper—the *Observer*. I told all my colleagues that it was private, and could therefore not be subjected in any way to sanctions by public opinion. In this way, those who offered to assist me felt quite free to express their views in the *Observer*. Not to let the *Negro* die, however, I kept the Chief Editorship.

I felt inspired by the setting up of the *Observer* to study the differences between Pan-Africanism and Pan-Arabism, or Pan-Islamism. I tried to make it very plain that the Southern Sudanese Africans aspired to the former while the Northern Arabs aspired to the latter. The Northern Sudanese students did not like this frankness, and some began to suggest that we should break away rather than federate, while others insisted on a policy of assimilation so that the Southerners and the Northerners would one day aspire to one nationality. I welcomed the first suggestion, and rejected the second on the grounds that our struggle was no parallel to that of the American Negro, where the Negroes were struggling for civil rights. Ours was a struggle for political freedom. I said I would even prefer to see a separate university built in the South for the Southern students rather than struggle to remain in one university with the Northern Arab in Khartoum, as did the American Negro facing humiliation in Little Rock. After this article all the university wall-papers, some of which had directed their attacks on the military junta of Abboud, were banned.

During my final year, I wondered what I was going to do after graduation, since I rejected the idea of serving an Arab Government. I discussed the matter with several of my colleagues, some of whom thought I was crazy. One of our ex-Members of Parliament, Mr. Elia Lupe Baraba, offered to raise capital for me to start a furniture business, since I had a great deal of training as a carpenter, and loved to practise it as a hobby. I was already set for this when two months before the examinations, the university advertised the post of a research assistant to conduct a survey on shifting cultivation in the South. I seized this opportunity, applied, and was accepted, having made up my mind to resign, and stay in the South when the time came to return to Khartoum to compile the findings. While working for the university in the South, I developed a great deal of interest in the district and the people. The work also happened to be in my own district and village. At the end of the field work, I decided to join the Blue Nile Cigarette Company—a subsidiary of the British American Tobacco Company. Apart from office work, my field work afforded a continuation of the research I had conducted for the university.

Perhaps one of the reasons for the District Commissioner's continual suspicion about my presence in the district was due to the sacrifice I had made in giving up my research job for a lower probationary salary for a period of six months. The District Commissioner made no secret about his feelings. Once, he stopped me in the street, to tell me that I was a waste to the Government because I had joined the private sector where my qualifications were not necessary. Moreover, he added, it was most strange these days to see a young man of my age and calibre working 'in the bush'. I reminded him that he was a graduate, working for the Government, and 'in the bush'.

I was all the time conscious of police surveillance which was carried out surreptitiously through secret agents— sometimes using my own clerks and labourers—best known to Southerners as 'C.I.D.s' or 'beggars'. These secret agents were always forced into making up stories, since they were paid only for 'bringing accurate reports'. No doubt their employers were sometimes embarrassed when they received reports saying I had given my friends a lift in a 'Government car', because it was not a Government car, and if it was, this could hardly have been a crime if my opposite numbers in the Government who were Arabs did so freely. Yet these agents were unavoidable since every educated Southerner was subjected to the same sort of surveillance.

On 19 January 1963 I was arrested, apparently to satisfy the District Commissioner, Mr. Osman El Naw, that he was supreme in the district. When I asked for the charges, I was told by the Police Inspector that 'the magistrate', that is the District Commissioner himself, was on trek, and had issued the orders for my arrest. To assure me that he had nothing to do with it, the Police Inspector showed me the signature of the D.C. on the warrants of search and arrest. This was the situation I had seen so many Southerners in before, and I knew that I could easily be kept in the cells without trial until the D.C. was either able to fabricate a charge, or was satisfied that I had been sufficiently tortured to come out of jail as a flatterer—having fully recognized his authority. I therefore decided to go on a hunger strike until charges were laid against me. On the third day of my strike, the Prison Officer appeared in front of my cell and read from a small piece of paper in his hand containing 'the charges'.

One was that I had something to do with 'disturbing public peace and tranquility', and the other was that I had 'published some false information with the intention of endangering the existence of the state'. Although this did sound as if I had been charged, I was not satisfied with the fact that the charges were read to me by a prison officer who normally dealt with convicted prisoners. I therefore preferred to continue the strike until I was satisfied that I had been charged by a magistrate. On the evening of the fourth day, I was escorted to the police office where I saw my boxes and piles of books and files on the floor. Some of these files contained unused questionnaires which, as they were of no value to anybody after my research, I had left in the village, and the police had gone all the way to collect them. I was asked such strange questions as why I had not handed these files to the district authorities when I decided to join the Tobacco Company. I only wondered why I should have handed them to anybody if the university authorities who had employed me did not need them. In the end I was told that although 'the main charges' for which I was arrested could not be substantiated, the authorities were convinced that there was something they needed to prove, and this could best be done while I remained in jail. This had something to do with my typewriter, university lecture notes on political science which mentioned Marx and the U.S.S.R., and some books on Marxist theory. I thought there was no point in arguing with the police officer because he would have been ignorant of what was taught at Khartoum University. So I returned to my cell, optimistically hoping for a release order as soon as the D.C.—who was said to be a graduate—had returned from his trek. On the fifth day I therefore abandoned my strike. If I had not kept asking to see the D.C., my presence in jail would have been virtually forgotten.

On the seventeenth day, I was escorted to the D.C.'s Office, and, to my surprise, told exactly what the police officer had told me. When I told the D.C. that I had brought all these books from university, and that what they contained comprised a large part of the economics syllabus, he said it was not his job; the police wanted proof. The Police Inspector, who had all the time tried to dissociate himself from my arrest, looked very embarrassed, and requested my release on bail. The D.C., convinced that I could not understand Arabic when spoken in a fast manner, said 'In spite of all these?'—pointing at the books. The Inspector replied, 'Yes, these can be taken care of easily.' I was therefore released on bail by a Northern colleague of mine in the Tobacco Company because I foresaw that conditions might one day force me out of the country before trial, which anyone knew would never take place. Being an Arab, he was the only person who would not be convicted. In June I was shown a confidential letter regarding the failure of the magistrate to charge me, and asking the Police Headquarters whether at least some of the books I had were illegal. Bank officials who had agreed to be agents were also told to keep an eye on my accounts in case I was planning to leave the country. Fortunately the bank was no more than a clearing house for me because I was engaged in opening a coffee farm. Having heard that the Anya-Nya—Southern Freedom Fighters—were about to strike, I decided to leave the country for the Congo, where I lived for a year before leaving for East Africa.

IV | The Anatomy of Domination

The most common questions which face dependent states are whether they can be economically viable without the continuous assistance and guidance of the parent states on whom they depend, and, if the country is rich, whether the local personnel will not let things slide into chaos. Records of balance of payments are produced either to support the argument that the colony is too dependent because of the amount of money that has to come from the Colonial Government to cover annual deficits, and can therefore not stand as an independent state, or to explain a favourable balance of payment by attributing it to the high standards of the expatriate staff. Sir Roy Welensky's case for Malawi (then Nyasaland) to be tied to the Federation was, as he claimed, that the Federal Government had to pay £3½–4 million to cover her annual deficits.

In the Southern Sudan the problem facing the Africans is no more complex than this. It is true that the backwardness of the Southern Sudan is a legacy from the British. The Gezira Scheme, which is the backbone of the Sudan's economy, was started with a loan of £E3 million approved by the British Government for irrigation and railway schemes, after acquiring £E1 million from private sources for constructing the Sennar Dam. The Condominium administration started off with Egyptian finance, and its first own budget in 1899 showed a revenue of £E8,000 and an expenditure of £E221,000. Deficits were incurred until 1913. Instead of allowing Egyptians to control the Sudan because Egypt covered all her deficits, the British decided to borrow money for the Gezira Scheme. That the Scheme is in the North is a sheer coincidence. It was never intended to be a Northern asset. What is surprising is that the British should have argued that the North 'should have some say in' Southern affairs because they were 'paying some £E900,000 in 1947 to make up the deficit on Southern revenue'[1] from money, which was largely acquired from the Gezira Scheme, while the same logic did not hold for Egyptian–Sudanese relations.

We have been told for ten years that our backwardness is a legacy from the 'imperialists'. It has taken this ten years to extend a railway line from Kordofan province to Wau—mainly for strategic reasons—and to develop the growing of rice on a small scale in Aweil where Southerners are forced to play the role of labourers. The reason for not developing the South always remains the same. *It is because the South is underdeveloped.* For what else is it when you tell people that one thing cannot be done because of lack of communications and good roads, and another is not feasible due to lack of trained staff?

The Chairman of the Jonglei Investigation Team wrote that 'given the money, the technical know-how and experts, the Southern Sudan could easily become one of the richest countries in Africa'.[2] We, as well as the Arabs, are well aware of this. But because we do not want to give them the chance to become settlers in order that they may supply their country from the proceeds of our land, they prefer to use their political power to prevent any development at all from taking place, even if it would result in adding some income to the Khartoum treasury. For the sake of brevity, I will mention only four of the many applications and economic undertakings which the Arabs have suppressed in the South for political reasons.

---

[1] See p. 27.

[2] The Jonglei team recommended in 1946 that a canal diverting the waters of the White Nile be built from Jonglei to near Malakal, in order to reduce the loss of water by evaporation in the *sudd*. This would provide more water for irrigation projects, particularly in Egypt. The project would involve profound changes in the lives of perhaps one million Southerners. See 'The Equatorial Nile Project', *Sudan Notes and Records* (Vol 32, 1952).

1. Messrs. Bauxal & Co. applied to undertake sugar production in the Southern Sudan. After some preliminary difficulties in convincing the Government, it was agreed that sugar plantations would be started at Mongalla and Malakal, and a sugar refinery would be constructed in joint partnership with the Sudan Government. Investigations and experiments were carried out at Mongalla, and, according to the Company's consulting engineer, Mr. N. Habif, they could aim at 20,000 tons of sugar a year at a cost of about £S4 million. The Arab Government, then under Abdalla Khalil, suggested that the factories be installed in the North and the sugar cane be transported from the South for processing. This proposal was obviously too expensive for the Company. While discussions dragged on, the army took over and cancelled the whole project on the grounds that it would entail the resettlement of 5,000 to 6,000 persons. This argument does not seem plausible; all it really reveals is a desire to maintain the economic *status quo* in the South. In the end, the Mongalla sugar project was moved to Gineid and Kashm el Girba in the North in order to give livelihood to displaced citizens from Wadi Halfa, despite the fact that sugar cane does not make a very successful irrigated desert crop.

2. In 1959–61 a German firm applied to utilize the papyrus of the *sudd* region for paper production. The firm proposed to construct a factory at Malakal, but the Arab Government insisted that the factory be built in the North in order to overcome *their* unemployment problem. After fruitless efforts to convince the Government that the factory must be built near the source of supply of the raw material, the project was abandoned. An Arab confessed that 'the papyrus in the South could produce all types of paper which will not only satisfy the home market and be the saving of millions of pounds, but will become an important export product, especially the paper pulp and cellulose. Other possible uses of papyrus are the production of fuel briquettes, alcohol, acetone, building board, pig and poultry food and plasters.' In May 1964, General Magboul el Amin declared: 'Japanese experiments [on paper and cardboard production

from papyrus in Upper Nile Province] proved highly successful.' Nevertheless, the Arabs simply decided to have their own paper factory in Aroma, using cotton stalks for raw material.

3. Plans for a fish-canning plant for Malakal were shelved, but later these plans were resumed in Jebel Aulia in the North.

4. Instead of accepting an application for the establishment of a meat factory in Bahr el Ghazal, the Arabs argued that it would be more economical to improve the Kosti meat factory. They also maintained that there was difficulty in disposing of the Kosti canned beef, and an additional factory would only add to the problem.

As has been mentioned, Northerners maintain this economic policy only in order to ensure perpetual political domination over the Africans. As far back as 1962 it was suspected that the Blue Nile Cigarette Company (a subsidiary of the British American Tobacco Company) which grew its leaf in the South and manufactured cigarettes in the North, would soon be forced to transfer even the growing of the crop to the North. 'Experiments' were being carried out in Roseires by a member of the management staff, and although money would have to be spent on irrigation, there was every indication that the continuation of the tobacco-growing industry in the South was endangered. Events moved too quickly, however, for an orderly transfer of the company to the North. In 1965, when the entire countryside came under the control of the Anya-Nya, this last commercial enterprise in the South was abandoned, leaving behind a very large tobacco crop.

In many cases it can be said, with a fair amount of justification, that Arabs deliberately try to impose a state of abject poverty and misery on the Africans in the South. For instance, in the year 1957–8 the Lakes District Rumbek (Bahr el Ghazal Province) was famine-striken due to the effects of a drought. People died in hundreds, while Aweil District in the same province produced dura (a type of sorghum) in excess of local demand. But the Arab administration imposed restrictions on the movement of dura from

Aweil District in order to open up a market for dura from Gezira and Gadaref in the North. On another occasion, when there was a severe famine in 1963–4 at Bor, the Government refused to allow international relief organizations to help.[3]

In 1960, I discovered that most of the dura in Maridi and Yei Districts (in Equatoria Province) which was being sold at about 50 piastres (about 10 Sudanese shillings) per petrol tin was purchased from the villages for only 17 piastres (just over 3 Sudanese shillings). On bringing the matter to the District Commissioner, Mr. Yusif el Mufti, he summoned an Arab merchant whom he described as 'most notorious' and would try to gain at anybody's expense. The merchant admitted buying dura from the natives but said he could not remember how much it cost because each native fixed his own price. When I asserted that the natives had no standard measurements, but that the merchants imposed their own, he admitted this but insisted that some natives were more sophisticated than others, and the merchants had to change their measurements accordingly. The District Commissioner then assured me that he would take up the matter. When I returned to the District in 1961, no change had taken place, except that the price of dura was rising in the towns while the price at which Arab merchants collected it from the villagers remained the same.

The implications here are manifold. The local people are discouraged from growing a surplus of dura or any crop for commercial purposes. On the other hand, those who live in towns are forced to buy the crop at exorbitant prices, thus remaining poor (they always form the lower income group). The beneficiary is therefore the Arab, whose quest for wealth is always aimed at improving his social status 'back home' in the North.

Except in a few cases, Southerners are generally denied trade licences for the same reasons as the whole South is denied economic progress. I was told in Yei by the same District Commissioner that Government policy was to encourage people who had some money to use it for tilling

[3] See Henderson, op. cit., p. 192.

the land rather than giving them trading licenses to open small bush-shops. I thought this was unfair because there was plenty of evidence to show that our best farmers are these small bush-shop owners who can employ labour. My own experience as a farmer and a small bush-shop owner is that both enterprises are interdependent, and more easily lead to success when the entrepreneur begins with a shop than with a farm, because of the time factor involved in waiting for crops to ripen, and the uncertainty regarding output in relation to investment. I believe these facts are well known to everybody.

Financially, the Sudan as a whole is among the poorest countries in Africa, and appears to be the most chronically insolvent. Its present budget is about £S60,000,000, 40 per cent of which is derived from direct taxation, to which the South contributes in the form of poll-tax, fixed on every Southerner from adolescence to a year or more after death. Twenty per cent comes from indirect taxation, such as customs duties and tariffs. As these are always transferred to the consumer, it is hard to see how it is argued that the South does not contribute. The rest is derived mainly from the Gezira. A very small percentage is derived from other types of trade, and some of the commodities which swell this trade, like hides and timber, are transferred from the South and taken for granted as being from the North before export.

There are no accurate figures for expenditures available. But, as can be seen, the South must appear on paper to be the most expensive region, with 20,000 Arab occupation troops stationed there, and all Arab policemen and administrators receiving standby allowances—the least, for a private, being 25 piastres (5 Sudanese shillings) per day. It was said in 1965 that a monthly record of £S2 million was being spent in the South on these 'security operations'. Having seen the administration, I would hardly doubt that this were true. I have seen a five-ton military carrier escorted by an armoured car and a scout car driven for thirty miles or so to get a packet of cigarettes for a military officer.

Perhaps one of the most constant reminders in the South of

the slave trade is the African labour force. A scheme laid down by the British, which is faithfully followed in the South by the Arabs, while changes are taking place in the Arab North. Southerners are paid a daily wage of 7 piastres (about 1 Sudanese shilling and 40 cents) in big towns, and 5 piastres (about 1 Sudanese shilling) in small towns and the rural areas, while the lowest wage in the North is 25 piastres (about 5 Sudanese shillings) for the same type of job.

Compulsory labour is also used by private Arab enterprises. In 1959, an Arab landlord who could not attract labour on to his farm deceived the villagers, saying that he would pay them double the normal Government wage. At the end of the month he told them that it was not easy to 'go against the government'. When they decided to leave, he reported the matter to the police and many of the 'ring leaders' were either badly flogged or imprisoned. The rest were forced back to work on the farm.

Under a scheme to 'raise the standard of living' in the district, the administration went round forcing local people on to private as well as Government farms leaving 'one male per family to cultivate for them'.

The difficulties any member of the Southern elite faces is that he is bound to find this system intolerable, and this is interpreted as inciting public discontent. A Zande ex-Member of Parliament, Mr. Samuel Renzi, was banished from his home for five years just for advising the administration to be more diplomatic in using forced labour.

Many political struggles in Africa have been a direct result of the land problem. The Kenya freedom campaign emanated from the fact that the sons of the land were pushed into 'reserves' to give room for 'settlers'. In Rhodesia, Joshua Nkomo describes it as 'the paramount issue in our struggle; the source of all our bitterness'. In the Southern Sudan, the Arabs have not followed the usual settler practice of first occupying the land and then legalizing their action later. They straight away displace the African from his land, using his own crops as a test of its fertility.

The land problem in the Southern Sudan is not as critical as it is elsewhere in Africa. In fact, I would have been inclined to describe it as non-existent if the Arabs had only respected the tenure system. Ordinarily, a Southerner regards land as a 'free gift from God' or 'God's land'. Land within the tribal boundaries belongs to the tribe collectively. An individual only 'owns' land which he has developed or has indicated his intention to develop. A foreigner may settle anywhere on tribal land provided he does not interfere with other people's belongings and also undertakes to pay his poll-tax to the chief. It is in contravention of this very loose concept of land ownership that the Arabs have acted. Arabs come to the South with the idea that all land belongs to the Government, since Southerners make no open claim to it.

The history of the Zande Scheme illustrates this conflict. Proposed in 1943 by J. D. Tothill, the Director of Agriculture, the scheme had as its economic backbone the production of cotton, but was a plan for resettling 180,000 people, involving schools, health services, and communications. The Scheme was started in 1946 with £S1,000,000 capital and, by 1952, 40,000 Zande families were farming cotton and coffee, each family being allotted thirty to forty acres. There was in addition a cotton ginnery, a sugar factory, and a textile mill in Nzara capable of producing 3,000,000 yards of cloth a year. In 1959, however, Northerners started to flock into the South to acquire the land of the Zande Scheme for coffee plantations. In Yei and elsewhere, Arabs who acquired land through the normal tribal channels described above went ahead quite peacefully. But some, mainly those who had been accustomed to exploiting Southerners, preferred to rob the people of their partly developed land. Chief Möri was jailed in Yei in 1960 for protesting against the use of force to acquire land from the people after they had put in so much energy and, in some cases, money. Mr. Elia Lupe, an ex-M.P., was also summoned by the District Magistrate to answer charges brought against him by Arab informers that he had instructed the villagers to obstruct the acquisition of land by Arab settlers.

Perhaps the system of land robbery which causes these incriminations deserves mention. In Yei, all the Northerners looked for was a 'good piece of land'. As I have said, the fertility of the land was sometimes judged by the quality of crops it produced. Many people were simply told that the land was wanted by the Government to whom it belonged. The system in Yambio was devised to remove the people to certain locations chosen by the Government under a 're-settlement scheme'. The Azande, who from time imme-morial have never lived in villages, were supposed to be clustered into Arab-manipulated 'model villages'—for ex-ample, the 'Abu Ismail village'. If the Scheme had been allowed by the Azande to succeed, it would have given plenty of room for Arab settlers.

However, the majority of the Northerners left in 1963 and 1964 because of the activities of the Anya-Nya, and in 1965 the Government even threatened to dismantle the machinery of the textile industry and ship it to the North. Today, nothing at all remains of the once-flourishing Zande Scheme except empty fields and deserted houses, the people having all retreated into the forest out of the reach of the Northern soldiers.

EDUCATION IN THE SOUTH

To deny anybody education is to deny him the very sense of personal values and self-improvement. A denial of educa-tional opportunities can therefore only lead to bitterness, for education is a self-propelling process which, once started, must not only continue, but must do so progressively.

The Condominium régime's neglect of education in the South could have been based on two main excuses. First, until 1930, the Government was preoccupied with the pacification of the South, where tribes were hostile to it. Secondly, until about this date, there was a general lack of resources—human and material—in the Sudan. Education was therefore completely entrusted to the missionaries, who had been given a free hand in the South, and were prohibited to proselytize in the North. The expulsion of Egyptian staff from the Sudan and the determination to maintain the policy of separate administration for the South, however, dictated the need to train 'local boys'. Hence, in 1927, the

Government decided to subsidize approved mission schools. But it was not until 1944 that the first Government elementary school was built in Tonj (Bahr el Ghazal Province)— mainly for sons of chiefs and their relatives. In 1948, the first secondary school class was started in Atar (Upper Nile Province) which moved to its proper buildings in Rumbek (Bahr el Ghazal Province) in 1949. Today, Rumbek Secondary School remains the only academic secondary school on paper for the four million black Africans of the Southern Sudan. A few hand-picked students are taken to continue their education in the North.

As was stated earlier in Chapter 2, the British moved very slowly with education in the South. The purpose of this was to preserve the pristine structure of tribal life, as the following quotations show.

The dominant theme of government policy has always been: do not detribalize; make each boy a better member of his tribe. . . . Choose candidates for post-E.V. [Elementary Vernacular] education for character rather than intellect. . . . Since this higher education is chiefly needed for those who will become leaders of their people, only boys of proved character and ability should be accepted for it. . . . Limit post-E.V. education to the needs of Government, trade and Mission employment . . . on the grounds that higher education is bound to detribalize.[4]

Perhaps more than anything else this attitude of the British administrators towards education is responsible for the sad lack of political leadership in the South from 1947 to the present day.

When the Sudan became independent in 1956, mutual distrust and social and political friction had accumulated for eight years between the Africans of the South and the Arabs of the North. The fire that had been kept smouldering under the policy of separate administration was lit ablaze on 18 August 1955. Independence was therefore seen by many Southerners as an aggravation of the situation, while the Arabs felt confident that it would give them absolute power to extinguish the fire. Like their predecessors, they set

[4] J. B. Bowers, *A Note on Missions and Education Policy in Upper Nile Province* (Civil Secretary's Office, Sudan Government Archives, 1942).

H

about 'pacifying' the Africans. But unlike their predecessors, they only managed to create an uneasy peace, since they deliberately exaggerated the situation in order to justify stationing occupation troops in the South.

For the Arabs, therefore, education was merely an avenue for a peaceful assimilation of the Africans while the army of occupation stood by to coerce when necessary. The first step taken by them on attaining independence in 1956 was to nationalize all mission schools in the African South. I am not against nationalization as such. What I am certainly against are the political motives which underlie Arab educational policy in the South. The Arabs believe that by converting the whole population to Islam they will secure not only loyalty but political docility among the Africans in the South. The difficulty of implementing such a policy is that it was imposed on a population already hostile to Arab rule, and well acquainted with Arab mentality. It was therefore destined either to fail, or to bring education to a standstill (as it has in fact done).

'Nationalization' meant no more than the confiscation of mission schools in the South by the Government in order to spread Islam—(the so-called 'national religion')—for polital reasons. In the words of Ali Abdul Rahman, the then Minister of the Interior in an Umma–P.D.P. coalition:

It is my government's concern to support religious education, and that is clearly shown by the progress by the Religious Affairs Department and the development of Ma'ahads [Islamic Schools] under its aegis.[5]

This has resulted in the virtual denial of education to the South. Islamic religious schools were built irrespective of the needs of the people and with the obvious determination to coerce Christian children into them. For instance the *Ma'ahad* built in Yei (Equatoria Province), to mention only one, was of no practical value to the people of the area. All the students in it were either practicing Christians or from Christian families. Parents often had difficulty in finding

[5] Address to the second sitting of the first session of Parliament in 1958 (Sudan Government Publication).

their children in these schools when they visited them. One parent, Mr. Fuljencio Lado, visiting his son John, was told that there was no student by that name in the school. After some time, one of the students discovered from Mr. Fuljencio Lado's second name that the boy he was looking for was *Mohamed* Lado. It was then that the boy was identified and brought to see his father. Such incidents have a disheartening effect on parents, children, and genuine educators alike; yet the Arab Government is determined to pursue its declared policy. As things stand, the South can expect no attempt from the Government to expand education unless it submits to Islam, Arabization, and political tutelage. The experience of the subjugated Africans in the Closed Districts of the Northern Sudan, like the Nuba and the Fur, however, makes the idea of being resigned to such a fate unattractive.

When independence was attained, the South had one academic secondary school at Rumbek with two streams. Since then, the Arab Government has only managed to add another two streams to the school—which has, at any rate, been closed, like all Southern schools, since October 1964 for 'security' reasons. Prior to independence, there was a commercial institute, known as the Juba Training Centre, which trained clerks, book-keepers, medical assistants, and sanitary overseers. This was closed and replaced by Juba Commercial Secondary School in 1955. So far, all that the Arabs have done is to add one stream to this school. A Malakal Secondary School exists on paper as window-dressing for foreigners who read about progress in the Southern Sudan. The fact about this school is that it was opened in Omdurman in 1962 with an intake of eighty students, only twelve of whom were Southerners. These twelve boys have remained the only Southerners in Malakal Secondary School, which has been absorbed into Wadi Seidna Secondary School and should now have over 3,000 students on its roll book. The Maridi Institute of Education, which was created in 1953 to replace Bussere and Mundri Teacher's Training Colleges, was transferred to the North in 1956. Since then, intake for Southerners has diminished so much that in 1965 there were only fifty-seven Southerners out of 103 students. There are no technical secondary schools in the South.

Girl's education in the South reveals perhaps the most pathetic aspect of Arab policy. Before independence there was an intermediate school at Maridi which was closed for eight years under Arab administration. It was, however, reopened in 1963 and closed again in 1964. At secondary level there are nine Government girl's secondary schools in the North with twenty-one streams, as against none in the South.

TABLE I

GOVERNMENT SECONDARY SCHOOLS FOR BOYS IN THE SUDAN—
SHOWING EXPANSIONS

Period	No. of schools in North	No. of streams in North	No. of schools in South	No. of streams in South
Before Independence	4	14	2	3
Added after Independence	18	45	nil*	3
Total	22	59	2	6

* Malakal Secondary School is included in the number of Northern schools.

In addition to these Government schools, there are a number of private secondary schools in the North (including Christian mission schools) with about forty streams for boys and over ten for girls. Private schools are not allowed in the South.

Needless to say, Khartoum University is entirely dependent for its recruitment of undergraduates on the output of secondary schools. There are now over 3,000 students in Khartoum of whom only about a hundred are Southerners. Discrimination within the university is most frustrating. More than three years lapsed from 1953 before a Southerner was taken into the faculty of law, and after him, the intake has been so regulated that there are no more than four Southerners out of fifty students. Intake for a Southerner into the medical faculty has become virtually a matter of luck. In 1959, for instance, only three Southerners were recommended for the interview. One of them had not asked to join that faculty and another had not even registered for that year's faculty examination. It was therefore clear that the intention was to take only one, although there were more than five Southern students who had applied.

In addition to facilities for undergraduate studies at Khartoum University, thousands of Arabs who fail to obtain places in Khartoum are granted foreign scholarships. Since independence, no more than ten Southerners have had this chance, and they were mostly sent by their departments on staff scholarships.

The usual argument for retarding education in the South is that the security situation there has not been conducive to progress since 1955. But the fact that two Ma'ahad el Ilmi (Islamic) secondary schools and six Ma'ahad el Ilmi intermediate schools and hundreds of Khalwas (Islamic schools) have been built within a period of seven years casts doubt on this argument. The real answer lies in the North's desire for political domination.

THE PUBLIC SERVICES

There is not a single aspect of life that is unaffected where politics is calculated to privilege one race at the expense of another. Priority to the privileged race is usually one of the most obvious features of such a society. Even colonial régimes always tend to pick out a race, tribe, or class for special treatment, either because of the colour of their skin, their loyalty, their social status, or may be simply because of human nature. As time rolls on, what is obvious nepotism tends to develop into a racial philosophy that justifies or rationalizes discrimination. In the Southern Sudan, considerable light is thrown on to Dr. Kwame Nkrumah's dictum: 'Seek ye first the political kingdom and all will be added unto you.'

It all really began with the British who made you a headman if they found you wearing a hat and carrying a stick, and would send your children to school or even respect you if they discovered that you already used spoons. We have already seen how Southerners were kept back in order to effect a low wage in the South. The effect of the policy of 'keeping these boys [Southerners] on probation at £S18 per annum for a considerable period'[6] was that when Arabs of the same educational qualifications were earning somewhere between £S510 and £S625 per annum, their colleagues in the South barely reached the £S108 and £S165 per annum scale. If they have been kept at the level of typing, tracing correspondence in the files for the British administrator, and stacking files in the offices and archives, then one is entitled to ask why.

When the 800 posts were to be Sudanized, only four Southerners who already qualified for promotion benefited. By the simple process of this social logic, it was absurd to promote a Southern administrative assistant earning between £S165 and £S180 per annum to the post of District Commissioner where he would earn between £S900 and £S1,200, or a Southern sergeant major then earning £S5 per month to a police inspector earning about £S40 per month. But it was perfectly all right to move an Arab staff clerk from one provincial headquarters to become Deputy Governor in another, or send Arab corporals and sergeants on six-month courses for promotion to police inspectors, just because they were already socially respected for their handsome salaries or because (in the case of the staff clerk) their salaries were only a scale below the step they were to take. I was told by a British member of our company staff that he thought a certain Southerner, who is now District Commissioner, could not do his job because he found him drunk (while on leave). He further thought, having seen this D.C.'s father and home, that it was ridiculous to give a man of such 'poor social background' a position of responsibility such as he held. 'It must be a sudden change for him to come from nothing to an A.D.C.' (as he then was). 'And', as if to make me feel inferior, he added, 'his father is a chief. I don't know what one can say about the others.' This particular expatriate appeared highly impressed by an Arab member of the staff who used to take him to his house to show how nicely he arranged his furniture, and, above all, to show that he ate good food. If we had stayed long, actual output of work for the company would have taken second place.

Our case is like putting two poor runners together in a relay race. One hands over late, and the other will not make up the time. The British were late in training Southerners to take up responsible posts in their country. We have seen some of their reasons, and now we should try to understand why the Arabs will not make up for it.

We have already seen, apart from historical factors, that the Afro–Arab conflict in the Sudan is the result of a struggle for political freedom by the Africans. From when the British started to transfer power to the Arabs until today, Africans in the South have been seeking political liberty, while the Arabs have persistently stood against their claim. One of the immediate arguments, again, has been that the South lacks personnel to effect a clean take-over. It is an argument used by all colonial régimes to prolong their grip on a country. Unfortunately, there is no known solution in the case of the South, because we knew that the Arabs will never discard such a valuable weapon. Since the Southerners already claim to be a different people, to train them will simply result in a transfer of power. Such a transfer of power is feared to have many evil repercussions by a nation which has long been playing the role of master. The obvious evil is the renunciation of power and privilege over the subject people—a thing which rarely comes voluntarily. The other evil is revenge, and the fear of revenge is clearly shown when we look at the number of Southerners taken into services like the police and the army. The figures in Table 2 speak for themselves.

TABLE 2

INTAKE TO THE SUDAN POLICE COLLEGE

Year*	No. of Northerners	No. of Southerners	Total
1950	10	3	13
1951	14	4	18
1953	13	7	20
1957	27	3	30
1960	29	nil	29
1961	36	1	37
1963	26	1	27
1964	35	2	37
Total	190	21	211

* There was no intake in 1952, 1954, 1955, 1956, 1958, or 1959.

Table 2 not only shows a clear case of discrimination, but it will be seen that before the transfer of power to the Arabs in 1956, thirty-seven Northerners had been through the Sudan Police College as against fourteen Southerners—about 27 per cent. Since independence, 153 Northerners have gone through the college, as against only seven Southerners—about 4 per cent. Apart from the officers passing through the college, the adoption of Arabic as the official language has enabled many Arabs to attain promotion through the ranks, since they then become more than just literate. But only five Southerners have been promoted this way, either for acting as *agents provocateurs* for the Northerners, or to enable them to retire on a reasonable pension as a window-dressing to attract the loyalty of others. There were only fourteen Southern police officers in active service in March 1965, and since then two are known to have been killed by the Arabs. How many remain now, I do not know. It is like asking how many birds remain on a tree after throwing a stone and killing two.

All the Southern prison officers were trained or promoted before independence. There were eight of them before the

Mahdist massacre in July 1965. Two of the most senior ones have been killed and one had to abscond to save his life. The remainder? I do not know.

The above being facts about minor security forces, we need not expect any miracles in the army. In fact, the highest rank held by the five top Southerners in the army in 1965 was that of major. The rest were captains and below—the majority being lieutenants (see Table 3).

TABLE 3

OFFICERS COMMISSIONED IN THE SUDANESE ARMY

Date Commissioned	No. of Southerners	No. of Northerners	Total
27.7.1954	I	19	20
1.8.1955	3	45	48
1.4.1956	3	35	38
1.7.1957	3	40	43
1.5.1958	2	58	60
1.5.1959	I	56	57
1.5.1960	2	58	60
1.1.1962	nil	64	64
1.1.1963	I	56	57
1.1.1964	nil	71	71
1.1.1965	4	67	71
Total as at 1.1.1965	20	569	589

Apart from the commissioned officers, promotions from the ranks are effected from time to time. Since independence, no Southerner has had such a favour, while by 1962 sixty Northerners had been promoted in this way. The situation before independence was seventy-seven Northerners and eleven Southerners; of those eleven, only two were still in active service in 1965. Two were executed in 1956 and the rest were dismissed after serving various terms of imprisonment for the 1955 uprising.

The impression one gets from observation is that Southern officers now in service are confined to purely instructional responsibilities. They are neither in the field, nor are they sufficiently trusted to have administrative jobs in their units. At the same time, they are constantly under supervision and must serve in the North since it is feared they will abscond and fight against the Government.

These facts apply to all Government services. In public administration, the stagnation of promotion of the first Southern A.D.C.s and the reluctance of the authorities to take Southerners has a discouraging effect even on believers in union with the North. Since independence, Southern administrators have been marking time at lower posts, with the result that the two highest of them are Deputy Governors. Arabs who were as far as two or three batches behind them have attained the status of Governors, and because more provinces cannot be created at home to absorb them, they are mostly sent out as foreign envoys. There is only one Southerner in the Sudan Foreign Service who was recruited in 1964 as a Third Secretary. Of the two Southerners in the Ministry of Finance, only one has reached the executive or decision-taking level. There is no Southerner in the Ministry of Commerce, Industry and Supplies. There is not a single Southerner as a Permanent Under-Secretary or Director of any department. This is not because there are not qualified Southerners, but because factors like the sudden introduction of Arabic as well as direct nepotism have retarded their promotion. The only Southerner, now Third Secretary, in the Foreign Service could not get Government employment after obtaining his Bachelor of Arts degree in 1962. He spent that year teaching in a private school. The only job Southern graduates are taken into with open arms when there are vacancies is teaching. This is obviously to the benefit of the Northerners since there are only two secondary schools in the South.

Clearly, then, all the discriminatory practices that are noticed in the economic, social, and political spheres are most heavily felt in the public services. Today, we have just enough civil administrators to run the South. Those who should now be in responsible positions have been deliberately shut out. When I was in the tobacco company, for instance,

my Arab colleague, who was senior, once assumed office
when we were left alone with him. He deliberately excluded
me from any administrative work in the office, thinking that
I would then remain inexperienced and be kept behind.
As is the practice among Arabs, he boasted about this all
over the place until I was eventually told by another Arab
about it. '*Kulu haja fi yedi. Oliver ma'a a'ndu haja.*' This means
literally, 'Everything is in my hands. Oliver has nothing.'
When the manager came back from leave, I confessed
frankly that I had learned nothing. I thereupon received
special coaching. But this was in the private sector with an
expatriate boss. My countrymen in the same situation in
Government service where the bosses are Arabs have
remained marking time, either to be dismissed as hopeless or
unable to claim promotions. Obviously, the answer is to
win the political kingdom and manage our own affairs.

SOCIAL IMPLICATIONS OF ARAB DOMINATION

'At least there is one improvement we [the Arabs] have
brought to the South: that is prostitution.' I was told these
unforgettable words by a university student during a discussion on the South. This is the type of outlook that under-
lies our social relations with the Arab North. As reported
by the Commission of Enquiry into the Southern disturbances in August 1955:

It is unfortunately true that many Northern Sudanese, especially
from among the uneducated class, regard the Southerners as of
an inferior race, and the Gallaba [Arab traders] in the South
form no exception to this, and often call the Southerners *abeed*
[slaves]. This practise of calling Southerners *abeed* is widespread
throughout the three Southern Provinces. It is certainly a
contemptuous term, and is a constant reminder to the Southeners
of the old days of the slave trade.[7]

No one would have had the idea of referring to a social evil
such as prostitution as an 'improvement' unless he felt he was
talking to an inferior.

The historical evolution of this outlook is straightforward.
The South was opened up by a variety of nations for the same

[7] Loc. cit, pp. 123–4

reasons: trade in ivory and slaves. Beginning with the Turks, then the Arabs of the North, trade motives soon gave way to organized slavery and exploitation. Attempts by other nations to suppress slavery towards the end of the nineteenth century met with failure because, as I have heard many people say, 'Slavery is in the blood of the Arabs'. Although we have no evidence, the mysterious disappearance of many Southerners who were either said to have been taken by Belgian cannibals (known to the people as *kulia batu,* i.e. 'man-eaters') or described as 'gone to Uganda' (which to the native implied 'no return') might confirm M. François d'Harcout's report that 'Arabia is still wrapped in the slumber of the dark ages'. This author, writing in 1962, goes on to tell of how 'entire cargoes of human merchandise arrive from Eritrea, *the Sudan* [author's italics], the Somaliland Coast, Afghanistan, the Indies and even the Far East. Some land at Djeddah, others on the Coast of Oman.'[8] Thousands of Africans from the South have disappeared in the North in this way, and relatives are made to believe that they had become adventurous due to bad city influence.

During a tour of his province, Mr. Ali Baldo, then Governor of Equatoria Province, asked the chiefs in Yei to tell their people not to discourage their daughters from having sexual intercourse with the Arabs because they (the Arabs) would 'not take the children [resulting from such an intercourse] when they return to the North'. These children, he said, would replace so many of 'your people who were killed during the disturbances in 1955'. I was told that a similar speech was delivered in all the districts.

One of the factors that makes social fusion between South and North virtually impossible is that centuries of Islam have created a deep sense of universal brotherhood among Northerners which impels them to resent any culture that does not emanate from their religion or is not imbued with it. The Africans of the South, on the other hand, have a mixture of indigenous pagan and Christian culture. Although Southerners are far from being 100 per cent Christians, it is surprising to see the degree to which Christianity has

[8] *News of the World* (London), 12 August 1962.

influenced the average man's way of life. For example, most villagers rest on Sundays and consider it a sin to do any work on this day of the week. I have also seen pagan families in the villages decorating their houses with flowers and palm leaves at Christmas. In most cases, my investigations have revealed that they have not seen the inside of any church. It is also amazing to hear stories from the Book of Genesis and the New Testament being related by these people without sometimes knowing that they are Bible stories. Most familiar are the stories of Adam and Eve, Moses and the children of Israel, the Holy nativity, and some of Christ's miracles.

These differences are taken by the Muslim North as 'imperialist influence' calculated to breed hatred between the Arabs and the Africans. Such an attitude and open intolerance by the ruling North makes social harmony impossible. On the contrary, an infamous piece of legislation known as the Missionary Societies Act, 1962, was enacted in order to eradicate Christianity and ensure the spread of Islam. It is generally believed by the Arabs that when the South has become Muslim, their political and social domination will be ensured.

The low income factor has a pathetically retarding effect on the social progress of Southerners which Arabs and other foreigners do not appear to understand. I was once asked to give my views on what percentage of their pay my workers (earning 6½ piastres—about 1 Sudanese shilling 30 cents per day)—spent on drinking *marissa*, a native liquor. I said it was anything from 60–100 per cent of their wages, and explained that all these workers have their cultivated plots on which their families really depended. Some of these local liquors are very cheap. This goes a long way to explain why many of our young men have become addicted to drinking, thus rendering some of them incapable of attaining rudimentary standards of apprenticeship which would qualify them for better opportunities. Instead of looking objectively at the causes of such social evils, Arabs simply brand Southerners as 'lazy'.

Whereas there is a natural tendency on both sides—Arab

and African—to keep aloof, the Arabs would like to see a situation where they alone would segregate against the Africans while the Africans crawl on their knees for integration. As a friend of mine once put it, 'They want you to be nice to them when they are not nice to you.' They will complain if you do not visit them or salute them in the streets. But they will never take the initiative to visit you, and only in very exceptional cases will they say 'hullo' to you before you do so. When you mix with them you must be careful, because their only desire to talk to you is to discover your political views and incriminate you. This is the situation in the Southern Sudan, and I believe not even an optimist can anticipate any immediate change.

With the present armed rebellion and political developments, things are bound to get worse than I have already described them in this book.

V | What Does the Future Hold?

THE NEED FOR AN INDEPENDENT SOUTH SUDAN

It is obvious from the foregoing chapters that both the Arab North and the African South will have enormous advantages once they part in peace. The sooner they part, the greater these advantages will be on both sides. It is also clear that the immediate beneficiary to such a partition would be the North. There is no question of stability and inability to manage a good government here. The Northerners, it is true, are as much disorganized and unable to maintain unity among themselves as many young African States. But I sincerely believe that left on their own, without having to bother about the South, they would very quickly head towards stability. Here I wish to state that I am arguing for a Southern State that will include the Nuba, the Fur, and possibly the Ingesena, who are an inalienable part of the Southern Sudan, if the North is to be the stable, pure Arab state I have in mind. But, of course, I believe in first setting our own house in order; then we shall see what direction the political thoughts of the Africans in the North will take.

Dr. Arnold Toynbee, Professor Emeritus of London University, rightly described the Sudan's case as freedom without justice.

In retrospect, we see that British policy in the Sudan was inconsequent. Before granting independence, she shielded the South against being penetrated and assimilated by the North, and thereby enabled the South to begin to develop on separate lines. Having done this, Britain ought surely to have given the South its independence as a separate state.[1]

[1] *Sunday Nation* (Nairobi, 17 October 1965).

Dr. Toynbee also rightly argues: 'The Muslim North is so much stronger than the pagan and Christian South that giving freedom to the Sudan has meant leaving the South at the North's mercy.'[2]

The spirit of the universal brotherhood of Islam with which Arab nationalism is highly imbued, the use of the Arabic language, and other cultural similarities in the Arab North are factors which would quickly work towards stabilizing that state. From a purely political point of view, the Arab North could more easily make up her mind as to whether to remain a separate state or unite with the United Arab Republic—a possibility which is presently made too remote by the fact that the South does not subscribe to this view, and therefore embarrasses genuine Arab believers in a union with Egypt.

Economically, the North could pull her resources together and concentrate them on her own development. The desperate efforts being made to grow citrus fruit in Gadaref and the Northern Province, as well as the Northern determination to experiment with tropical or semi-tropical crops such as sugar cane and tobacco in the arid North, because of uncertainty about the South's future, reveal that the North could be self-sufficient even with regard to agricultural products. On the other hand, there is the possibility that potential entrepreneurs in the North could invest their money in agricultural projects in the South. All this, of course, depends largely on how quickly the South becomes independent, so that relations between the two states do not deteriorate to the point of no return. If the South is left to fight too long and too hard in order to win her independence bitter memories may jeopardize future co-operation. A friendly, land-locked, but potentially rich Southern neighbour might be an asset to the North, and not only will the valuable money being spent on military suppression be saved, but more money would be earned through the rail outlet to the Red Sea and through direct investment. It would also be possible, as Southern delegates proposed at the Khartoum Round Table Conference on the South, to

[2] Ibid.

work out closer ties than those which exist, for example, among the East African countries in the East African Common Services Organization. Here, the North has an additional advantage over the South because she has a monopoly of trained personnel who would not only dominate the management of such arrangements for a long time to come, but would guarantee a cultural spill-over. Finally, the North would be released from her present task of crushing African culture and replacing it by an Arab way of life. This is indeed an abuse of public funds, especially when we all know that a military victory for the North is impossible.

The advantages of political independence for the South are obvious. No country can know its limitations if all its wealth is controlled by a foreign state. We do not pretend that we are a wealthy nation. But what we need to have is our own government that will assess and admit our own poverty. The ordinary Southerner in the village pays a poll tax without anyone ever explaining to him why he has to. Many parts of the South have no roads, no dispensaries, and no schools—services for which these taxes are levied. It is true that these cannot be achieved overnight even by an African Government in the South. But it is sometimes consoling to the man who pays these taxes to see the face of a Government representative who will explain these taxes, and why it is necessary to pay them. Unfortunately, the Arab administrator thinks this is too condescending. Chiefs are used for extorting taxes, and are held responsible for any failures to do so.

The Africans in the South also need to progress. But this progress will be of little benefit if it does not incorporate some of their traditions. The Arab desire in the South has been to erase African traditions and transplant their own before any conscious attempt is made towards developing the country. In so doing, they also transplant some of their uncertainty and all the reactionary ideas that are an essential part of their culture and character.

To have our own government is to be able to control our own resources and plan accordingly. We do not need to hide the fact that the Arab Government is paying large sums of money to cover deficits in our budget. I hope they will also be honest enough to accept the fact that some of this money comes from Britain, Egypt, the U.S.A., and Yugoslavia (especially during the military régime) to cover the over-all deficit. But the point I should like to make clear is that a country's path to political liberty cannot be determined by its amount of wealth. Were that the case, the Sudan would perhaps have been among the last in the queue for independence in Africa, and I imagine the queue would have been headed by countries like Zambia and the Congo (Kinshasa). The Sudan's adverse balance of payments was only nearly corrected by the military junta. Debts still stood high—although a claim to have reduced them to just over £S2 million was made in 1962. Nevertheless, the Sudan is still an independent sovereign state. It would seem then that the balance of payments does not rule a country, and a country does not automatically renounce its sovereignty because of an adverse balance of payments.

Let us now turn to the economic prospects of an independent South. I have seen many fish-producing camps in Equatoria Province, and I have been told that there are many more in Upper Nile Province. Bahr el Ghazal Province also has a number of them, especially, as the name indicates, in the Lakes District. The management is placed in the hands of the Fisheries Department and the poor output corresponds to the lack of managerial skill coupled with lack of interest on the part of the fishermen, who are very poorly paid—1 Sudanese shilling or 1 Sudanese shilling and 30 cents per day. Yet 605 tons of dried fish were produced and actually exported from Upper Nile Province from only thirty-five camps, according to the *Daily Mail* (London) of 28 February 1962. It is highly probable that the output would be immense if these fishing camps were run on a co-operative basis, and only put under the general control of the Fisheries or Game Department. The Congo is a ready market, and if further surpluses could be produced, the market could be extended to the Central African Republic, and so on. Unfortunately, the Arabs are decidedly against co-operative movements in the South. The question that lurks in the mind of an Arab administrator in dealing with any type of association is that of security and subversion. A Southerner who is sophisticated enough to think about a co-operative society is thought to be politically minded enough to wish to overthrow the Arab régime in the South. To allow him to form a co-operative organization is therefore considered tantamount to allowing him to form a political party.

It is indeed surprising to see that a country which had attracted so many traders for its ivory in the past should fall into such commercial obscurity. We read so much about ivory without hearing about or seeing it on an economic scale. But we know that certain *jallabas* assemble tusks almost gratis for export to the North at exorbitant prices. Indeed, the African South is immensely rich in fauna. Here is what the Sudan *Almanac* of 1962 says:

The main shooting area of the Sudan lies to the South of the line made by the rivers Bahr el Arab, Bahr el Ghazal and Sobat. Between this line and the Kenya, Uganda and Congo frontiers lies a vast country teeming with game. . . . Juba lies in the heart of the game country.

Tourism could therefore be another valuable industry in the South if she were freed of all her uncertainties.

Although it is said that the South is poor in mineral wealth, perhaps the small gold-mining areas in Equatoria Province could be expanded. During my research work, I collected some information from the dusty, yellowing files in the archives in the Government's office in Juba, and from that information it would seem that many river beds in Equatoria Province contain gold. It is also an established fact that the South has plenty of iron ore deposits which the people had smelted for many years before the advent of outsiders. This could acquire economic importance if coal were acquired on a large scale for smelting.

By far the most important, however, is the South's agricultural potential. Cotton, coffee, and tobacco have already been launched on a commercial scale, and have all proved to be most successful. Rice is more widely grown in Bahr el Ghazal Province than is needed for local consumption. Cocoa and rubber experiments in Yei and Yambio were described as successful, but no effort has been made to introduce them on a wide scale. The fruit of the mango tree grows wild in most parts of the South, and could provide enough raw material for a canning plant. In fact it is difficult to think of any tropical or sub-tropical crop that will not grow well in the Southern Sudan. With proper management, there is plenty of good soil all over the South that will favour a wide variety of crops. Irrigation would only be necessary around the borders with the arid North (i.e. from latitude 11°N), there being plenty of rain in the other areas. Indeed, in many parts there is too much rain, and drainage projects would be necessary.

One of the earliest proposals in Yei District was to fell timber on a co-operative basis. I talked with some of the leading contractors, including Dada Awu, and it appears that the desire to pool their resources together to form a co-operative was very strong. But the administration would not allow any form of association, and instead, much time was spent going round persuading individuals to be content with their personal efforts. In the process, individual grievances were exploited and a false competitive instinct created.

These examples could go on almost *ad infinitum*. My objective here, however, is not to boast about the South as a potentially wealthy state. The point I wish to make is simply that the Africans in the South need to be given the opportunity to make their own trials and errors. Under an alien Government, reluctant to develop the South because of political uncertainties, we have no chance. An independent state, on the other hand, is as fully responsible for its economic chaos as it is for any success and good planning. We in the South are perfectly aware of possible failures. But come what may, we must be *free*.

THE SOUTHERN SUDAN AS A STATE

There are so many speculations about the future of the

Southern Sudan—as there usually are about any country struggling for independence—that I feel fully justified in making some predictions. We have been asked whether we think we can succeed or not. Fear has been expressed that the South has no binding principles and no single leader to make the emergence of a stable state feasible: 'another Congo' is feared because it is thought that the only factor binding the Africans in the South is their hatred for the Arabs of the North. Then there is the question of trained staff for the management of the civil services, the nation's treasury, and so on. Even the type of government contemplated by the freedom movement becomes the subject of much controversy. Will the state turn communist, capitalist, or African Socialist? For even the 'non-aligned' or 'neutral' young nations have aligned sympathies. If the Southern Sudan becomes free, will she not join East Africa and add her voice to Black Africa? On the other hand, what will be the fate of the Arab North? Will she not give herself up to the communists (which sometimes only means Nasser's Egypt) in despair? These questions, together with the contention that the Southern Sudan case is a 'minority' problem, which if solved by granting independence to the South would open up a number of similar problems in Africa, may need more elaborate and more academic answers than I am able to give here.

The question whether the Southern freedom movement can succeed or not is closely bound up with the preceding chapters. No genuine nationalist movement can fail. It can be suppressed, no doubt, but it will always come back in another way or take another form, and suppression itself acts upon it like an electric charge. The obvious answer is therefore in the affirmative—the Southern Sudan will be free. Twelve years of suppression and military rule, coupled with memories of the last century in the South, are in themselves enough to keep the struggle an ever-growing, burning reality. There is no logic in expecting a people to surrender their national aspirations in favour of external rule. Where a people's national sentiment belongs is not a matter of debate. It is instead a phenomenon to which unqualified respect is due. We feel African, and demand to be treated as such. We have not been treated as Africans, and are being ruled by Arab governments from the Northern Sudan who believe in eradicating our African identity in order to perpetuate their rule. For this reason a national revolutionary movement has erupted, about the success of which no one should have any doubt. All talks about crushing it are therefore an illusion.

As a unifying principle we have our history, our common enemy, and our cultural similarities. We were enslaved together, we have fought together, and we are suppressed indiscriminately as a single subject race. I see no better binding forces than these. When we win, the victory will be ours, and we will reap the fruits together.

It is true that we have our differences. This does tend to prolong the struggle—it does not stop it. We all believe it is unfortunate. But then show us a single freedom struggle, or a single nation in the world, which has no differences. All I am saying is that differences are part of us, and as long as we do not postpone fighting the enemy to turn our efforts against each other, all these differences can be accommodated within the struggle, and may even act as a spur for eradicating the enemy. But in any case where no single person has attained the unquestioned leadership of a freedom movement—as did Kenyatta in Kenya, Kaunda in Zambia, and Banda in Malawi—sympathies are directed towards the principles to which the movement is dedicated. Once left to the people, the question of leadership will resolve itself. That was so in Uganda, and, I hope, it will be the case in Zimbabwe (now Rhodesia).

The Southern Sudan's case has very little parallel with the independence struggles of many other African countries. Except for a few coffee entrepreneurs and Arab merchants, we are not a settler-infested country. We have always felt different, and our struggle started right from the time there were signs of being thrown into a union with the Arab North. Our bitterness is against Arab rule, and there is no sign of our people ever refusing to accept experts from any nation to guide and advise our young government in the future.

Since the army take-over, Arab oppression in the South has only helped to give Southerners a sense of oneness, and we do not expect anything so drastic to happen as to shatter that sense. We believe whatever differences there are are slight, and can be solved by being handled together, even if it requires a certain amount of give and take, thus perhaps sacrificing the ideal. Kenya, for instance, had to start with strong regional assemblies and a relatively weak central government. On 12 December 1964 the position was fully reversed. Had Kenya's ruling politicians been too ambitious, and started off with the 1964 constitution, they would have pleased the prophets who anticipated chaos in their country after independence. A good government is one that starts from a broad basis, working inwards towards a strong central government. In other words, politicians must know the minds of the people, admit their limitations, and work to bring them together. Looking at Uganda today, this experiment seems to be the most perfect choice for young African states with a diversity of peoples. I remember a Ugandan saying to an Englishman at Juba, 'If you leave us alone, we shall know how to deal with our hereditary rulers. You did not bring them from England, and we are not going to suggest that you take them along.' Instead of eliminating hereditary rulers, Ugandans first created General Secretaries who are consitutional heads of government in places where there were none. There is no reason why the Southern Sudan cannot do likewise.

As has been mentioned earlier, the Arabs use the argument of lack of African staff and funds to administer a Southern state only as camouflage for their real motives— the desire to maintain exclusive opportunities for Arab staff, and the fear of revenge. So much is said about lack of staff, while nothing is done to remedy it, that the only conclusion open to an African is that he is cautiously being guided into second place for all eternity. There is no pretence on the part of the Africans that they could take over public posts at all levels. But the Arabs will even attempt to kill all those African public officials who pose as their prospective successors—as has been taking place since Mahgoub's Government came to power. The question of public services and public funds would therefore seem to be largely dependent upon the aspirations of the people and the integrity of their leaders. We are confident that the Southern Sudanese know what they want at all levels, and are definitely conscious of their limitations.

It may be premature, as some of my friends have suggested, to discuss the type of government the South will have. I quite agree with this view and hope my friends will forgive me for speculating on a future that might be remote. I feel there is room for satisfying the wishes of those who are inquisitive about the future.

A good government is one that knows its people and tries to accommodate their wishes in accordance with the country's resources. Whether to adopt communism or capitalism is not usually the choice facing leaders of a developing nation. In many countries of Africa the term communism has an unpleasant connotation, because it implies not only a system of government but also the regulation of individual conscience and belief, thus making it tantamount to a religion. It is therefore difficult to conceive any African state welcoming communism with open arms. Socialism, with its various prefixes (scientific, liberal, or African) is therefore the word to use and argue about. The other extreme, capitalism, is equally difficult to conceive in an undeveloped or developing country. Private resources are so limited or lacking that it would be suicidal to entrust the burden of the country's economy to the private sector. On the other hand, the young government might be paying for its services from foreign loans, and it would be unreasonable to expect it to take over or nationalize the entire economy. A wise government of a developing nation will therefore try to strike the balance somewhere in between. Where the balance is struck should depend on whether the largest proportion of the nation's wealth is in the public or private treasury. If both are lacking, then there should be no hesitation in welcoming foreign investment. All this should depend on the desired rate of growth. The application of this argument to the Southern case is very obvious.

In the Southern Sudan, both public and private funds are limited, if not lacking. What the nation will have to offer is therefore a plan, tailored to suit her situation and aspirations.

From a purely political viewpoint the South, as I see it today, must start off with a decentralized system of administration and the employment, where possible, of local agencies for the simple administrative needs of the country. An ambitious centralized system, though cheaper in the long run, might only discourage centripetal forces by creating pretexts for discontent. When people are given the chance to make their own trials and errors—which admittedly might be expensive—only then will they appreciate the absurdity of holding too tightly to their own, and begin to demand being more and more identified with their central government. It is my deep conviction that when a country gradually works from a decentralized towards a centralized system of government, the central government gains from the immense stock of experience which is piled up by the regional administration in carrying out their community development programmes.

Whatever a 'minority problem' means, I have my objections against the concept being applied to the Southern case. First of all, a minority problem implies a struggle for civil as well as political rights within a community. It further implies, in many cases, that these rights are or could be made legally available but are only being sabotaged by certain elements in the society—thus causing the problem to exist. In any case, the struggle is directed against discrimination, and attempts are usually made to strive towards equality within one society. This is not the case in the Southern Sudan.

A document made available at the Khartoum Round Table Conference on the South, headed *Population and Manpower*, says: 'About 311,000 Southerners proper [from the 1955–6 Census] are already in the North, and the flow continues. The movement in the other direction is relatively slower. The political instability in the South has discouraged population movement in that direction.' As I have said earlier in this chapter, we are not a settler-infested country. The Arabs in the South are not even immigrants in the proper sense of the word. They are administrators, officials, or merchants. What is more, they consider themselves as being in a foreign land, and expect to be treated so. Many schools were closed because Arab teachers did not want to work in the South. All this removes the Southern case from the category of a minority problem. The fact is that, as things are in the Sudan today, we have two countries, and one—the African South—is being administered by the other—the Arab North. To argue that the Sudan is to be recognized as one independent state is to slam the door on the sufferings of the South Africans, the people of Zimbabwe, and, whether we like it or not, Angola and Mozambique, which Portugal maintains are only 'provinces' of the mother land. They are not the first in the history of mankind to have 'their country' within the boundary of another. To recognize the Southern problem as a colonial case will therefore be a step in the right direction.

CONCLUSION

This book has described the historical process which has led to the Southern and the Northern Sudan being given independence as one country, and the misery this has caused. The sensible thing to do would be to let them part again in peace.

Appendix

When the Round Table Conference was adjourned, it was abundantly clear that the real core of the problem was the failure of politicians to agree on a constitutional formula. The Conference therefore agreed that a 'Constitutional and Administrative set-up which will protect the special interests of the South as well as the general interests of the Sudan'[1] should be formulated. A Twelve-Man Committee was subsequently appointed to investigate the possibility of such a set-up. The Conference agreed to reconvene as soon as 'the Twelve-Man Committee has finished its work and submitted its report'.[2] We may therefore consider the Twelve-Man Committee as another Constitution Committee in the history of the Sudan. Like its predecessors, it encountered many obstacles, and, according to the extract from its own document reproduced below, appears to have died a natural death two weeks before completing its work.

The Twelve-Man Committee's Report[3]

5. The Committee began its life with faltering steps.

It was not constituted until nearly two months after the Conference due to the engagement of the Government and the Parties in the General Elections.

And the controversies about the representation of some Southern parties in the Committee also occupied several meetings.

[1] *Resolutions of the Round Table Conference* (March 1965).

[2] Ibid.

[3] From a mimeographed report circulated by the Twelve-Man Committee in September 1966.

Thereupon the People's Democratic Party and the Communist Party decided to withdraw from the Committee.

And here the Committee faced the most critical period in its life, but in the end it decided to concentrate on its primary terms of reference: The Constitutional and Administrative set-up.

The Proposed Constitutional and Administrative Set-up

6. Although the Round Table Conference could not reach a unanimous resolution on the pattern of Government which should be adopted it did resolve that two forms of solution: Separation and the present *status quo* (Centralised Unitary Government) should not be considered by the Committee.

The Committee, therefore, after receiving the schemes submitted by the members, set aside those schemes which were outside its terms of reference. Then it found that the Constitutional and Administrative formula which it was trying to work out was of two main parts: The distribution of powers between the Centre and the Region and the relationship between the two, and further that its objective would be facilitated if the distribution of powers was considered first.

Therefore, lists containing the powers proposed to remain in the Centre and those proposed to be transferred to the Region were worked out from the schemes accepted by the Committee, and the study began.

7. The result was that the Committee were agreed that the following powers shall be exercised by the Central Government:

(1) National Defence

(2) External Affairs

(3) Currency

(4) Communications and Tele-Communications

(5) Foreign Trade

(6) Nationality

(7) Customs

(8) Inter-Regional Trade

8. The following powers were to be concurrent between the Centre and the Region in the following manner:

(i) Security Forces:

(1) The National Legislature shall by enactment, organise the security forces. This will include:

(a) Recruitment and Use of the National Police Force which carries out the functions assigned to such forces.

(b) The Recruitment and Use of the Local Police Force.

(2) The Head National Executive shall be the ultimate authority as regards the security forces and can in certain

circumstances place any of these forces under his direct command.

Subject to (1) and (2) above the Region shall recruit and use the local Police Force.

(ii) Education:

(1) The policy of education shall be National and in the hands of the Centre. Policy has been defined to include at least the following: Syllabuses, National Planning of Education, Definition of Standard and Qualifications. But as there are some regional peculiarities that reflect on education this fact must be given its due consideration in formulating the policy.

(2) That the administration of education up to the intermediate level should be the responsibility of the Region.

(3) And that it should be concurrent in the secondary stage so that the Centre and the Region may each establish such schools and administer them.

(4) That Higher Education (post secondary) should be in the hands of the Centre.

(iii) Public Health:

The Centre should retain:

(1) The General Policy and Planning.

(2) Education and training of doctors, the registration of doctors and all the other professions attached to the medical profession.

(3) Control and supervision of assisted projects.

(4) National Policy for Nutrition.

(5) Control over drugs and poisons.

(6) Medical research and control of epidemics.

(7) Registration of births and deaths.

(8) Hospitals: The licencing and the supervision for maintenance of the standards is the province of the Centre but the administration is concurrent, so that the Centre and the Region may each administer the hospitals established by it.

And the following to be transferred to the Region:

(1) Control of Endemic Diseases.

(2) Environmental Health Services.

(3) School Health Services.

(4) Health Education.

(5) Maternity and Child-Welfare Services.

(6) Control of Markets.

(7) Training of Village Midwives.

(8) Training of Medical Assistants and opening of Dispensaries.

(iv) Antiquities:

Both the Centre and the Region may carry on their own excavations.

(v) Labour:

(1) The Centre shall lay down the policy.

(2) The execution of the policy as laid down in the legislations should be by the Region.

9. The Committee agreed to transfer the following powers to the Region:

(1) Regional and Local Government Administration.

(2) Regional Public Information.

(3) Promotion of Tourism.

(4) Museums and Zoos.

(5) Exhibitions.

(6) Projects: Establishment of Local roads, maintenance of main roads, Town and Village Planning.

(7) Protection of Forests, crops and pastures—according to national legislations.

(8) Protection and development of animal resources—according to national legislations.

(9) Land utilizations and agricultural development in accordance with the national plan for development.

(10) The study and development of languages and the local culture.

(11) Commerce and Industry and Local Industries organization of markets, trade licences, formation of co-operative societies.

THE GOVERNMENT OF THE REGION:

A Legislative Assembly and an Executive Machinery

(a) The Legislative Machinery:

Each Region shall have its legislative body in form of an assembly elected directly on the same conditions as to qualification as that applied to the Central Parliament.

(b) The Executive Machinery:

1. The Legislative Council elects the members of the Executive Council for the Region. These are responsible to the Legislative Council which can dismiss them.

2. It was agreed that the Head Executive should be from amongst the inhabitants of the Region and he should be responsible for the Central Agencies and units in the Region by delegation from the Centre as well as for the Region Executive Machinery. This is to guarantee co-ordination and unity of leadership.

It was also agreed that this necessitates that he should be appointed through a joint process. But there was difference over the exact procedure to be followed.

There is a view that the Regional Assembly should offer two candidates and the Central Government should choose from between them.

And another view that the Central Government appoint him after consultation with the Region.

THE RELATIONSHIP BETWEEN THE CENTRAL AND REGIONAL AUTHORITIES:

We had to consider here how to strike a balance between preserving the sovereignty of the National Parliament to protect the vital interest of the Nation and at the same time securing the autonomy of the Regions and protecting them against any persistent and unwarranted interference by the Centre in their sphere of powers.

We would like to clarify that when our agreed system of Government is adopted as part of the Constitution, there can be no withdrawal of the Regional powers except by a constitutional amendment with a two-thirds majority. Further it is conceded that the Central parliament being sovereign—subject to the constitution—may over-rule any Regional legislation or take the initiative in legislating within the sphere of the Regional powers. But in order to protect the Regions against any unwarranted encroachments by the Centre we recommend that:

(*a*) A declaration be written into the constitution to the effect that this sovereignty is granted to Parliament:

(1) to protect the vital interests of the country, and

(2) to guarantee the co-ordination of Regional legislations and to provide leadership and initiative.

(*b*) Before any such legislation is passed by Parliament there must be full consultations with the Regions concerned.

Emergency:

(1) We were agreed that in the case of a public security

emergency occasioned by an external or internal threat the Centre may either suspend any of the Regional Powers or dissolve the Regional Assembly provided that in the latter case elections must take place within one month after the Emergency, and

(2) a declaration of emergency has to be approved by a resolution of parliament within two weeks of its announcement.

The Regional Geography:

After it had finished with the distribution of powers and the relationship between the Centre and the Region the Committee went on to consider the geographical location of the Regions.

(1) The Southern Members suggested dividing the country into 4 Regions:

(*a*) South (Constituting the present Southern Provinces).

(*b*) East (Constituting Blue Nile and Kassala);

(*c*) West (Constituting Kordofan and Darfur);

(*d*) North (Constituting Khartoum and Northern Provinces);

or to adopt the present division in the Northern Provinces making six Regions out of them and making the three Southern Provinces into one Region.

(2) The Northern members suggested adopting the present administrative boundaries for the Provinces creating nine Regions out of them.

(3) The Southern members gave the following reasons:

(*a*) Any division must start by the North and the South as two units because of the differences between them in culture, Religion, language and Race.

(*b*) The South considers itself as a unit and the Southern Citizens have expressed their wish to remain as a unit and there is nothing in this demand that is detrimental to the public interest. Also our basic duty is to solve the Southern Problem and this necessitates giving this fact due consideration and not treating the South as the other parts of the country where no such problem has arisen or not to the extent of the Southern Problem.

(*c*) The guarantees agreed upon for the protection of the autonomy of the Regions will not be sufficient unless we enlarge the Regions geographically so that the public opinion in them will carry such a political weight that the centre shall have to pay that fact due consideration.

In fact this was put as a condition by the representative of the Southern Front for his agreement to the relationship between the Centre and the Region agreed to above.

(*d*) The present administrative divisions are inherited from the Colonial Administration and are based on the tribal system and our duty is to adopt a system that weakens tribalism and so help Sudanese nation building.

(4) The Northern members based their view on the following reasons:

(*a*) It is preferable to begin by present administrative divisions. This facilitates administrative activities as the main advantage of Regional Government is that it limits administrative units to smaller areas thus avoiding administering large units from a far Centre.

The South from an administrative aspect is too large to be administered from one Regional Capital.

(*b*) It is true that we are primarily interested in the solution of the Southern Problem but we must take note of the repercussions of any solution that we propose. In view of existing claims for regional autonomy any scheme that we develop is bound to serve as an example.

(*c*) In substance the demand of the Southern Parties has been for a constitutional set-up that would enable local initiative for the advancement of their region. . . .

(*d*) If the South is made into one Region this will perpetuate the sense of confrontation between North and South which we are trying to end through these efforts. As there may be some sentimental feeling that urges this demand and as sentimental feelings can be legitimate and beneficial it may be met in this case by allowing any number of Regions to pool any of their services.

(*e*) There is no objection to any adjustment of regional boundaries later on if experience indicate such a change. Both sides maintain their stands on this point.

CONCLUSION

These are the broad lines of the proposed system of Government. The public opinion—which has been patient and understanding on our difficult task through a whole year during which we tried silently and persistently to find points of agreement, and during which we fluctuated between feelings of hope and despair—is entitled to know that a break-through has been made and to be assured that the remaining differences of opinion are not fundamental and can be solved.

When we have finished preparing our report within the next two weeks and submitted it to the Government so that it calls the Round Table Conference in accordance with the Resolutions of that Conference we will devote ourselves to our other terms of reference relating to the normalization of the situation in the South. We hope that we will find the sufficient understanding and co-operation from the Government that will enable us to carry out this duty and that the public opinion will give us its support and encouragement.

According to this document, it is clear that the failure of such bodies to find a solution is inherent in Sudanese politics. The South wants something in the form of liberty. Nothing in this document suggests secession. On the contrary, all one can see here is a very weak form of guided autonomy which the North can withdraw when it thinks fit. The North, on the other hand, tends to pitch its refusal on the assumption that if you give anything to the needy you only run the risk of increasing his demands. All efforts are therefore directed towards frustrating any demands from the South.

The 'All Parties' Committee

However, the desire for a dialogue continued to prevail on both sides. It was therefore thought, during Mahgoub's first Government in 1965, that an 'all parties' Committee should be formed to overcome some of the difficulties which had faced the Twelve-Man Committee after the withdrawal of the P.D.P. and the communist parties. This Committee was short-lived because it could hardly claim to represent 'all parties' when the parliament decided to ban the Sudan Communist Party. To overcome this difficulty, another committee had to be formed.

The National Committee for the Draft of the Constitution

This Committee was formed under the directions of Sayed Sadiq el Mahdi, who briefly succeeded Mahgoub as premier in 1966-7. It was at once different in outlook in that instead of seeking to solve the difficulties arising out of the Twelve-Man Committee's work, the National Committee evaded all its predecessors' recommendations. Further obstacles were brought in by trying to push an Islamic Constitution through this Committee. As is usual in South–North constitutional relations, the Southern Front boycotted the National Committee for a long time. The present draft to be presented to the Constituent Assembly is therefore an Islamic Constitution in broad terms. Whether or not it will be tabled before the Assembly remains to be seen.

Another Committee?

Soon after elections, every party seems to have reviewed its position. The U.D.P. controls 101 of the 218 Assembly seats. This means Mahgoub heads a cabinet which he can hardly control, while the U.D.P., on the other hand, cannot govern without the co-operation of the five Umma members of the Cabinet. The situation is therefore not only as fluid as it has always been, but a constitutional crisis is already being fostered by the activities of the political parties.

The most pressing problem currently facing the politicians is whether or not to set up another constitution committee. There are growing signs that a large number both inside and outside the Assembly favour the setting up of a new committee. While this problem remains unsolved, another one has been fostered. It is felt that the new committee should make a fresh start rather than consider the National Committee's recommendations.

Since the Round Table Conference

Thus, since the Round Table Conference, the Sudan has simply continued to assert itself as the graveyard of constitution committees without producing a single draft which is acceptable to all parties. One was formed by the parties after the Round Table Conference, and immediately Northerners and the Government objected to the seating of the two Southerners from exile (I was one). They managed to have substitutes to form the Twelve-Man Committee. The new

Twelve-Man Committee then agreed to the creation of an 'All Parties' Committee which was dissolved by Sayed Sadiq el Mahdi in favour of his National Committee for the Draft of the Constitution. We are now waiting for the fifth committee since March 1965.

With the North obviously uncertain (if not afraid) of the prospects of a permanent constitution and the South pressing for a recognition of the principles of self-determination for its population, it should not surprise anybody if the present Assembly (and possibly any successive one) comes to the end of its life without producing an acceptable draft.

To find a peaceful solution, I agree with Mohammed Omer Beshir (in his book *The Southern Sudan: Background to Conflict*) that the dialogue should be kept open. But the success of such a dialogue will largely depend on mutual respect between Northern and Southern politicians. If Northerners simply develop the idea that 'the majority of the Southern delegates proved to be uncompromising and bad negotiators; they lacked experience and tended to suspect the motives of the Northern leaders, seeing a pitfall in any move by the North', then fresh dialogues will be so prejudiced as to be of little use.

Experience and ability to negotiate cannot be taught. In political matters, *experience* is a relative term whereas 'it always pays to gain the confidence of the intelligensia whether they are fully educated, half educated, or quarter educated'.[4] We need not blow our own trumpets. Southerners feel that the problem is aggravated by Northern intransigence, since it is they who negotiate from a position of strength. Naturally, this has driven the South into thinking that the hope for salvation lies in attaining as much strength as possible. There may then be a compromise between might and might.

[4] *Report of the Commission of Enquiry . . . August 1955*, op. cit. p. 7.

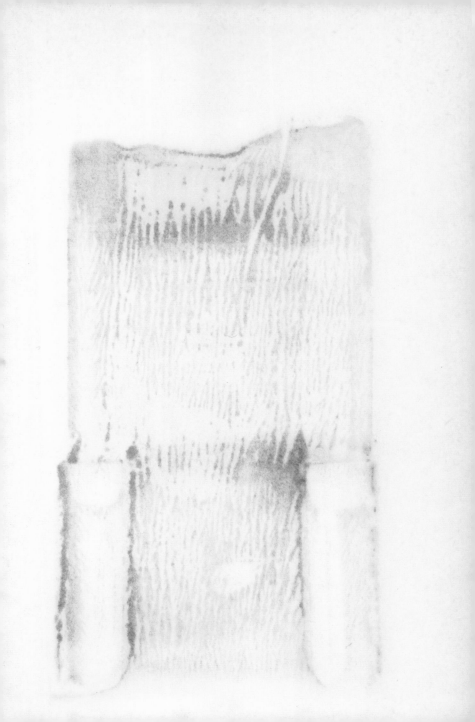

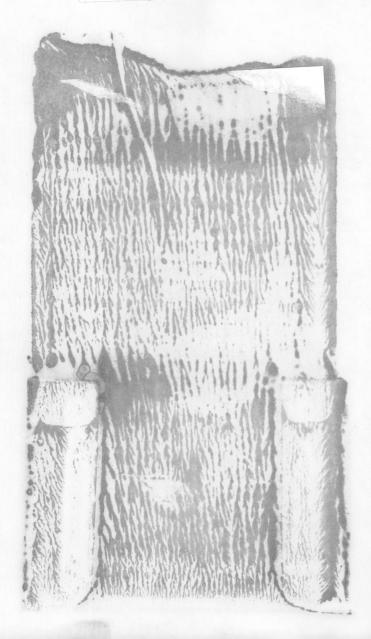